THE
LIVING
THEATRE

Pierre Biner | # THE LIVING THEATRE

Horizon Press   New York

Originally published in French under the title, *Le Living Theatre*.

Copyright © 1972 by Horizon Press
Library of Congress Catalog Card No. 72-171015
ISBN 0-8180-0501-7
Printed and Manufactured in the United States of America

PHOTO CREDITS

Jacques Dominique Rouiller: 1-13, 15-22, 24-38; Gianfranco Mantegna: 23; Ben Lifson: 41-47, 49.

ACKNOWLEDGMENTS

I want to express my warmest thanks to Julian Beck and Judith Malina for their complete and friendly cooperation. They gave me access to all of their records, including the sketch books and staging directions used in preparing their productions. I also wish to thank M. and Mme. Claude Vallon and M. Juan Bonal for their valuable help.

P. B.

CONTENTS

LIST OF ILLUSTRATIONS

1. *Mysteries.* The representation of harmony and collective beauty during the chord scene.
2. *Mysteries.* Death, vertical rigidity, and the military, as represented in the brig dollar scene. (Gene Gordon center stage.)
3. *Mysteries.* An arrangement of stiffened corpses in the plague scene. (Standing: Julian Beck as an undertaker.)
4–6. *Mysteries.* Three *tableaux vivants;* in #4, left to right: Luke Theodore, Cal Barber, Judith Malina, Gene Gordon; in #5: Sandy Linden, Steve Ben Israel, Jim Anderson, Henry Howard; in #6: Nona Howard, Rufus Collins, Rod Beere, Julian Beck.
7–12. "If we acted in costumes rather than in our street clothes, we wouldn't be ourselves. By wearing our own clothes, we are signifying that we are all inside society, like anybody else, and not the privileged, not the critics from outside. We are saying that we are part of society." 7. Rufus Collins; 8. Mary Mary; 9. Frank Hoogeboom; 10. Petra Vogt and Birgit Knabe; 11. Judith Malina; 12. Judith Malina and Isha Manna.
13. Julian Beck, January, 1968.
14. Sketch by Judith Malina for *Frankenstein.* The bottom half of this sketch indicates that Judith was originally planning to find a way to use a representation of the open eye on the scale of the representation of the Creature—that is, the entire height of the structure. It proved to be technically insurmountable to do both and only the Creature was incorporated in the set.

15–16. *Frankenstein.* The attempt to levitate has failed and the victim (Mary Mary) tries to escape but is trapped.

17. *Frankenstein.* The actors face the audience, sitting Indian-style. From left to right: Pamela Badyk, Steve Thompson, Julian Beck.

18. *Frankenstein.* Frankenstein about to remove the victim's heart. (Mary Mary and Julian Beck.)

19 and 22. *Frankenstein.* The Creature reduces the structure to a miniature by its monstrous size. In #19, Petra Vogt at the control booth, center right. (These particular pictures were taken during a Zurich performance on an extremely small stage where the backdrop could not be hung. Details are more visible in #24, *q.v.*)

20. *Frankenstein.* The inscriptions in English of the various parts of the head on the backdrop.

21. *Frankenstein.* Frankenstein paints the mystic signs on the corpse. (Frank Hoogeboom as the corpse, and Julian Beck.)

23. *Frankenstein.* The legend of Buddha, the Enlightenment. The control booth, A1: B1 is sending instructions.

24. *Frankenstein.* Three flashes light up the image of the cross of the Four Horsemen of the Apocalypse: four actors bundled in capes carrying representations of a horse's head. The Creature (Jim Anderson) can be discerned in center left, and Frankenstein (Julian Beck) below it as he is declaiming the hundred twelve-letter words. In extreme right, the control booth and the speaker (Pamela Badyk).

25. *Frankenstein.* Excitement inside the structure as the Creature (Jim Anderson) frees itself from the shackles that have bound it to the operating table in center left.

26. *Frankenstein.* Jenny Hecht, victim of the electric chair, during a break.

27. *Frankenstein.* The Ego (Henry Howard) has been expelled from the head.

to bottom, Carol Berger, Sandy van der Linden, Mary Mary. (Photograph taken at the American premiere in New Haven.)

42. *Paradise Now.* Rung 1 Scene 1. "Don't step on the Indians."

43. *Paradise Now.* Rung 2, Vision 2. Echnaton, Birgit Knabe, Jim Anderson, Henry Howard.

44. *Paradise Now.* Rung 4, Rite 4. Breaking the barriers of touch.

45. *Paradise Now.* Nona Howard improvising. Behind her, actors and spectators entwined.

46. *Paradise Now.* Rung 6, Rite 6. Pierre Devis as the "voyager" with Rufus Collins as the opposing force.

47. *Paradise Now.* Julian Beck in center.

48. Cartoon from *The New Yorker,* December 14, 1968.

49. In the waiting room, after the troupe debarked in New York. Frank Hoogeboom is playing the flute.

THE
LIVING
THEATRE

PREFACE

"Every time I accept a dollar bill from somebody or give somebody a franc, it's using the whole blood-money system, man-barter system, the war system, and supporting it. We are ALL owned by it. Every single move I make is a slave gesture to the system. The only way I could live and be decent and honorable about what I believe would be in jail, that is, under the direct, coercive brute force of this system."

Judith Malina spoke these words during the first few months of the Living Theatre's European exile. This statement points out clearly enough that all exclusively esthetic critical judgments about the company were inadequate. If there is beauty, if there is art in the company's presentations, it is to be regarded as a bonus. First of all, there must be dialogue. Talk. Saying "No!" to war, to all restraints on freedom, to all violence, no matter the cause it is used for.

This book is not a plea for the defense, it is not a court of judgment. It makes no conclusions. It is an account, stern and friendly. It is not didactic, and it is not an essay on the theatre.

Gathering documents for this account was the most pressing task. The documents contain a lot of lies. Deliberate, frequent lies. Cataloguing events is one of the ways to shut out life, to dispose of something bothersome. Once an illustrated French weekly distorted an interview with Judith Malina and Julian Beck. Although the interview had been conducted in the best possible atmosphere, the published version dragged them through the mud. They addressed a simple question: "Why?" No reply was ever received. There may well have been one, but one so essential that it could not be spoken. It had never reached the conscious mind, perhaps, and could not account for the explosion of hatred.

In *La Brûlure de Mille Soleils* filmmaker Pierre Kast tells the story of a man traveling through interstellar space who meets a young woman on another planet. He is at the point of possessing her when six beings appear. The lover understands too late that the six shadows are those of accomplices, not of judges, and that he thought it was possible to apply laws to an unknown planet when they are not even valid for every earth-being.

If the actors of the Living Theatre seem to be Martians, perhaps this is so because their world is to come. The voluntary exile in Europe precipitated the transformation. Nothing more.

PIERRE BINER

28 February, 1968

The original edition of this book appeared in French in April, 1968. It was revised, brought up to date and augmented by the material relative to *Paradise Now,* and a new edition also in French was published in March, 1970. This edition is a translation of the second (or 1970) edition. Chapter 42 was written especially for the American edition.

P. B.

1 | PREHISTORY

The adventures of the Living Theatre began with the first meeting of Judith Malina and Julian Beck. It happened in New York in 1943, when he was eighteen years old and she seventeen.

Judith was born in Kiel, Germany, but her family name hints at distant Spanish roots. Her father, a rabbi, had a presentiment of approaching disaster as early as 1927, and by 1929 the family was in America. Her mother had been an actress before her marriage, and Judith stepped on a stage for the first time when she was two years old.

Julian is also Jewish. His father's family was from Sambor, a city once part of the Austro-Hungarian Empire, now part of Poland. His mother was born in the States; her father had been born in Alsace, her mother was a first-generation German-American. Julian grew up in the middle-class environs of Washington Heights on Manhattan's Upper West Side. The Beck family seemed to have a propensity for teaching; many of them chose it as a profession.

Judith and Julian became constant companions in 1943, almost immediately after their first meeting, and in 1948 they married. They have two children; their son Garry is twenty-one, their daughter was born in July, 1967. They named her Isha Manna—Hebrew for "woman-manna" or "manna, made woman."

When they met they were both stagestruck. They went to see every play running in New York from Chinatown to Broadway, sneaking in during intermissions. They talked incessantly about poetry, theatre, painting, and literature.

Julian had dropped out of college in 1942 in the middle of a lesson. He had had enough of school, and he wanted to find his own environment outside the family. He was a painter; and a painter in New York. At that time painting was moving at a much faster pace than theatre. During the war New York was the meeting place of all the artists who had fled Europe. In 1945 Julian encountered Peggy Guggenheim, around whom gravitated the members of the Atlantic surrealist circle. He discovered Breton, Duchamp, automatism. He met Jackson Pollock, William Baziotes, and their friends in the New York School. In 1945 he exhibited at Peggy Guggenheim's. Julian was also writing. He was always writing. He took on all sorts of jobs for a living. The only thing that mattered was to be in New York, and to be free.

Judith began her theatrical studies in 1945 under the great Erwin Piscator at the New School Dramatic Workshop. She was the most conscientious student in attendance. "I am pretty sure that she recorded Piscator's lectures to the most minute detail," Julian remarked. (She was to become a scrupulous archivist of the Living Theatre as well, of course.)

Nevertheless, rapport between Judith and Piscator was not as deep as she would have liked. She was distressed, yet her will surmounted all obstacles; when she left Piscator after two years, she knew that she had not wasted a second of her time.

Julian was resistant to indoctrination, but he sat in on a three-hour course Piscator was giving once a week. Called "The March of Drama," it was an introduction to the interpretation of drama, ranging from Greek tragedy to contemporary works. (Julian was scandalized to find that Piscator concerned himself even with Noel Coward.) The students staged complete and complex plays, utilizing a variety of techniques Piscator had demonstrated for them.

Through this period, Judith and Julian worked in all kinds of jobs. On lucky days, Julian trimmed windows and Judith had small parts in television plays.

At the time Judith began her studies with Piscator, she was intent on becoming an actress. It did not take her more than two weeks to realize that directing fascinated her as much as acting. As for Julian, he had always wanted to be a set designer. In New York, theatre was synonymous with Broadway —an empire with locked doors. It was simply inconceivable to Judith and Julian to think of any theatre other than Broadway, at first. It was there they had to get a foothold. Still, Julian had been increasingly aware of how difficult that would be ever since 1943: "I began to realize that the theatre (. . .) had no place for me. (. . .) Judith was more tenacious. She insisted on working in the theatre, and if there was no place to work then she would make a place to work. She told me about this. There was no hesitation, of course, we would make our own theatre."[1]

They made their first attempt in the summer of 1948 in a basement on Wooster Street. The theatre was to be maintained on subscriptions. The repertory was to consist of Japanese Noh dramas translated by Ezra Pound, medieval miracle plays, Strindberg's *Spook Sonata,* Ibsen. They rehearsed and sold sixty subscriptions. Then the police came, thinking they had discovered a clandestine whorehouse. The theatre on Wooster Street never opened.

They had chosen the name "The Living Theatre" from among some fifty possibilities early in 1947. It was to be a "living" theatre, one that would emphasize contemporary plays performed in such a manner as to move the spectators. (When the Becks began staging plays in their apartment, for lack of suitable space after the Wooster Street shutdown, some wags attributed the name of the troupe to the fact that it was located in the Becks' "living" room.)

[1] Julian Beck, "How to Close a Theatre." *Tulane Drama Review,* Vol. VIII, No. 3, Spring, 1964.

Also, it was to be a repertory theatre, alternating a number of plays, affording steady employment to actors, changing the bill every night—in complete contrast to Broadway with its star system, its exhausting long runs, and the periods of idleness most actors were forced to deal with.

In 1947 Judith and Julian had stationery printed and wrote letters to everyone who seemed likely to offer them advice or support. They wrote to actors, directors, set designers, and also to writers, poets, painters, and dancers, including such eminent ones as Jean Cocteau, Paul Goodman, and John Cage. Many replied; Robert Edmond Jones, the great set designer, did even more. He invited the Becks to come and see him. The two meetings they were to have with Jones would influence their future decisively. But, at that point, the Living Theatre was still a dream.

2 | SIX THOUSAND DOLLARS IS TOO MUCH. . . .

At the time the Becks went to see Jones to tell him about their plans, they had not yet entirely abandoned their hopes of one day forcing open the doors of Establishment theatre. To say "Establishment" theatre—that is, Broadway and its counterparts in other cities—is not to say Establishment-supported theatre, by any means. In response to a questionnaire sent out by the Rockefeller Foundation as recently as 1963, only twelve out of the five hundred cities that replied were supporting some form of dramatic art. Of course in 1947 such subsidies were even more rare.

American theatre is run entirely by businessmen. Patrons of the performing arts do exist, but they are for the most part primarily interested in the opera. Universities assign an important role to dramatic arts, but then university theatres benefit from vast government subsidies, are not independent, and cannot really focus on producing for a wide audience.

The Federal Theatre, which operated from 1935 to 1939, was the only example of government subsidy to drama in America, and it owed its existence to the special circumstances of the Depression. Judith and Julian had not seen the Federal Theatre in action, but they knew what it had been about. They also knew there was no chance at all that it would be revived. Broadway was a target for valid criticism from their point of view, and the Becks were willing to try the repertory system to break in on and challenge it.

Robert Edmond Jones heard out the young

couple who talked so fervently. When they finished, he told them that his first impressions about them had been wrong. He thought they were ready to change the theatre, he thought they already had the answers, but now he saw that they had merely formulated the questions. He asked them how much money they had. They had six thousand dollars, inherited from an aunt of Julian's. "That's too bad," Jones said gloomily. "I wish you had no money, no money at all. Perhaps then you could create the new theatre." Why? Because art was not possible on Broadway. It was imperative to forget about plush seats, admission prices, large capacity houses. Nothing important could be done with that set-up, nothing would ever come out of it.

This was a successful man of the theatre speaking, the set designer for most of O'Neill's plays, the author of the respected theoretical work, *The Dramatic Imagination*. His advice to the Becks was to put on plays in studios, lofts, their apartment if need be—he even offered his own large studio for the purpose. "It's at your disposal whenever you want it. You can begin here."

Judith and Julian declined; it was not what they were looking for. It was to take them a long time to realize that Jones gave them sound and true advice. "But we were young; that's our excuse," they say today, with a smile. It took several years of experience before they were ready to adopt Jones's observations. Julian had not expected such a profession of faith from a man who worked regularly on Broadway and who had proposed, in a lecture at Yale attended by Julian, a "theatre of the subconscious" that would integrate Joyce's literary innovations with modern film techniques. It was that Jones who interested them, not Jones the dispenser of advice.

Time passed. Judith and Julian were searching tirelessly. They were looking for a theatre, for money, for actors, for technicians. Finally, having failed to find the ideal place, they decided to stage their productions in their apartment at 789 West End Avenue. Performing in their home for an audience of friends was primarily an affirmation of their all-consuming love for the theatre, and Julian freely admits that this love became a true obsession. He had revised an old pleasure, one fading from memory, but still of value and importance. "Ever since the age of four or five," Julian recalls, "I have been aware of an attraction to the theatre. When I was four, I used to imitate circus performances in the living room, to amuse my family. At six, I played in school plays, and I was taken to the opera and to plays. At seven, I wrote scenarios and school plays (. . .) and adapted them to be performed at home."

Julian then relates an instance of remarkable behavior that revealed to him, even as a child, that he possessed both a precocious moral altruism and an unconscious fascination with and trust in the power of magic. He must have been six years old when he was taken to see *Hansel and Gretel* at the Metropolitan Opera. When Hansel was called upon to eat on the stage, Julian, who had nothing but a handkerchief in his pocket, began to eat, too, and ate the handkerchief in its entirety. When his father caught sight of this, Julian was struck by the feeling that he "did what had to be done." He experienced in reality what Hansel experienced on the stage, and he too committed an ill-fated act (because the witch in the opera eats the gluttons). By having eaten his handkerchief, having exorcised evil by evil, Julian felt that "all the children were free, out of the oven, uneaten, alive. (. . .) The event convinced me of three needs in the theatre for total experience: physical participation by the spectator participant, narrative, and transcendence." Julian discovered that "you are what you eat, and what you won't eat any more."

The first performance by the Living Theatre was given in the Becks' apartment on August 15,

1951. Four short plays were presented: *Childish Jokes* by Paul Goodman, *Ladies' Voices* by Gertrude Stein, Brecht's *He Who Says Yes and He Who Says No,* and Lorca's *The Dialogue of the Mannequin and the Young Man.*

One finds clearly stated in their very first performance what were to be some of the Living Theatre's abiding interests: anarchism, poetry, Oriental theatre (via Brecht), improvisation, experiments with language.

3 | FIRST, CHANGE THE LANGUAGE

It is possible for one to trace, from the first performance in your apartment, a fairly clear tendency to reject a theatre of pure entertainment, to reject also a theatre of satire and show instead a preference for scripts that stimulate the imagination and are concerned with language.

JULIAN: We wanted to change the whole method of acting, but that cannot be done in one stroke. The language had to change, first of all. In our reaction against naturalism, against the American version of Stanislavski, we turned to the contemporary poets, to a poetic theatre. We wanted the theatre to accomplish a revolution, eventually, one that had already transformed the other arts—music, painting, sculpture.[1]

Were your intentions quite clear at the time?

JULIAN: Not as clear as they are today. We sensed—before we really understood—what was wrong in the American theatre. What we wanted to do most was to enhance the blossoming forth of poetry in the theatre, while preserving a certain realism, of course. The poetry of words, above all.

[1] Julian Beck quoted by William Glover in *Theatre Arts,* December, 1961: "We believe in the theatre as a place of intense experience, half dream, half ritual, in which the spectator approaches something of a vision of self-understanding, going past the conscious to the unconscious, to an understanding of the nature of all things. And it seems to us that only the language of poetry can accomplish this; only poetry or a language laden with symbols and far removed from our daily speech can take us beyond the ignorant present toward these realms."

You are extremely well read and you have seen untold numbers of plays of all genres. When did you encounter Artaud and Brecht, who influenced your work so strongly?

JULIAN: Artaud was completely unknown to me during the early years. As for Brecht, we were familiar with his theories mainly through Piscator. He was rarely performed. In 1947 Joseph Losey directed Charles Laughton in *Galileo* in New York. . . .

Did you see it?

JULIAN: I did, but Judith couldn't make it. It was extraordinary! I was completely carried away. . . . Judith met Brecht about that time at Piscator's, even though Brecht and Piscator didn't see eye to eye. . . . Max Ernst was there also. Judith laughs about it now, but she was more impressed by Ernst! I suppose that will give you some idea of the level of our development at the time.

What did anarchism mean to you then?

JULIAN: There were very few anarchists. Judith and I were already resolute anarchists. Paul Goodman was the most famous one. It was almost impossible to talk about political matters in the theatre, except in extremely guarded ways.

The example of the Federal Theatre must have inhibited people.

JULIAN: It has. Another thing about the Federal Theatre, I have been told, was their tendency to simplify. I think it is a terrible notion that a play has to be reduced to exaggerated simplicity if workers are to understand it.

How do you characterize your efforts in 1951?

JULIAN: I think that if our first productions had any style at all, you could sum it up in the word "honesty." But we were never satisfied, and we are never satisfied.

4

DOCTOR FAUSTUS

By performing in their apartment during the summer of 1951, Judith and Julian were following the advice of Robert Edmond Jones, at least. They were to follow it once more and perform in a loft for a year and a half in 1954-1955. The intervening period—and the last years in America—were spent according to the norms, with tickets being sold at a box office. The norms nevertheless included some important achievements: progress toward a type of collective direction, rotation of plays in repertory whenever possible, cohesion in the selection of plays.

Between their West End Avenue debut in 1951 and the opening of *The Brig* in 1963, twenty-two productions were staged, comprising twenty-nine plays—most in verse. None departed from the Becks' ideal, which was continually affirmed. Every production aimed at the expansion of consciousness by sustaining the boldest attainable realism or by serving poetic theatre or by reflecting the discoveries of psychoanalysis.

Apparently, at least some of the Becks' choices were made at the right time. Those who visited the new home of the young company did so because the Becks offered something valuable, something that was not being offered elsewhere. Following the premiere of the Living Theatre's first production in a real theatre, the Cherry Lane, in December, 1951, William Carlos Williams wrote the Becks a significant and prophetic letter: "It is so far above the level of commercial theatre that I tremble that it might fade and disappear."

This particular production was Gertrude Stein's

1938 play, *Doctor Faustus Lights the Lights*. Faust's beloved, Marguerite, dies and is sent to hell. Faust encounters Mephisto and asks him what sin he has to commit in order to join her. The answer is kill. Faust kills a dog and a little boy. Marguerite does not recognize him when he arrives in hell, for he is not the Faust she had loved.

Julian sees an essential kinship between this play and *The Brig*. Faust is inundated with electric light; it is the price of his soul; in *The Brig* it is the blinding light falling straight from the ceiling on the prisoners of the Marine Corps. Faust asks how he can get to hell, and he is told: by killing. Hell is the "brig," the prison for men who have been taught to kill.

The moral and philosophical concerns of *Doctor Faustus* intrigued the Living Theatre. Gertrude Stein, too, had been attempting to revitalize words, the literature of the first twenty years of the century, "a period (. . .) which tried to revivify language, which did revivify language, and with it the structure, the form of literature, by erasing the platitudes and exploring and pushing at the boundaries of meaning in writing."[1]

The language of *Doctor Faustus* is truly remarkable. Repetitions and assonances endow it with an almost hypnotic quality. For example, here is a brief excerpt from scene i. Faust chants: "I knew it I knew it the electric lights they told me so no dog can know no boy can know I cannot know they cannot know the electric lights they told me so I would not know(. . .)."

The originators of the Living Theatre speak very harshly about the early productions. They do not renounce them. For them it is simply a question of a whole other world. Fifteen years of a sinuous route, of researches and adventures; a constant outflow of

---

[1] Julian Beck in the introduction to Kenneth H. Brown, *The Brig*. New York: Hill & Wang, 1965.

energy and creativity, sometimes rewarded. The Living Theatre looks for solutions in all kinds of theatre.

In staging Kenneth Rexroth's *Beyond the Mountains* next, the Becks turned toward Japanese, Chinese, and Greek drama. The play was a verse adaptation of the *Oresteia,* and it was exceedingly long—one reason for its failure. It simply did not fit into a single evening. The actors wore masks, and Tei Ko choreographed Noh dances to specially composed music. *Doctor Faustus* had been an indifferent success, but *Beyond the Mountains* was an embarrassment. Judith said later that the two most notable failures in the history of the troupe had been *Beyond the Mountains* and, years later, *The Women of Trachis*—both adaptations from Greek classics—and that failure had to be ascribed to the *mise-en-scène* in both cases.

Julian's six thousand dollars had evaporated by this time. The Becks wanted to do Paul Goodman's *Faustina,* but it was impossible to stage a Roman fresco without money. Instead, for the cost of thirty-five dollars (!) they put together a bill consisting of a repeat of Gertrude Stein's *Ladies' Voices,* T. S. Eliot's *Sweeney Agonistes,* and *Desire Trapped By the Tail,* an irreverent diversion written by Picasso in 1941. The bill had the overall title "An Evening of Bohemian Theatre." It proved to be the company's first real success; the paying public was coming. The actors, who had not been getting any pay, received a generous share of the receipts; they were quite content.

Money in the box office now enabled the Becks to produce *Faustina,* Goodman's modern verse adaptation of a legend dealing with the wife of the Emperor Marcus Aurelius. The troupe still cherishes the memory of a very successful moment where the scenery of Roman architecture disappears as the civilization it represents crumbles. Then, in a startling change to the present, Faustina walks toward the audience across a totally bare stage and says, with deep conviction, "We have enacted a brutal scene, the ritual murder of a young and handsome man. I have bathed in his blood and if you were a worthy audience, you'd have leaped on the stage and stopped the action."

The last production at the Cherry Lane was Alfred Jarry's *Ubu the King,* and, as the curtain raiser, John Ashbery's *The Heroes. Ubu's* production cost was even lower than the thirty-five dollars spent on the "Bohemian Evening." The sets were made of brown paper, the costumes of rags; half the actors slept in the theatre, and all of them performed without pay.

Ubu was accepted, but not *The Heroes.* Its language was colloquial, and certain "clinical" allusions to homosexual love provoked sometimes vehement protests from the audience. Whether by coincidence or not, the Fire Department decided just then that the theatre was a fire hazard and ordered it closed down after only three performances. The Becks had to start again from scratch.

All in all, the Cherry Lane represented an important period for the troupe. There, for the first time, the dream of a repertory theatre had been fulfilled. For four weeks "An Evening of Bohemian Theatre" and *Faustina* were presented on alternate evenings. There, too, the Becks inaugurated the Monday gatherings; performance was suspended and poets, writers, and playwrights congregated to read from their works and discuss their current projects. Dylan Thomas and John Cage were among the first who were invited to read and speak.

5 | MISS STEIN AND MR. WILLIAMS

How do you feel about your first real theatre, the Cherry Lane, now?

JULIAN: We had rented it during the summer of 1951 for six months or a year. [In March, 1951, Judith had made her directorial debut at the Cherry Lane off Broadway with a play written by a friend; it was called *The Thirteenth God,* based on the life of Alexander the Great. Judith played the role of Alexander's wife, and Geraldine Page played a prostitute named Antigone. The play lasted two weeks and was a catastrophe, but from it came the Becks' decision to rent the Cherry Lane on a long-term basis.] Our third production, "An Evening of Bohemian Theatre," was unexpectedly successful. The reviews were not exactly good, but at least they made an impression on the public. Almost at the same time another company, the Circle in the Square, attained a big success with Tennessee Williams' *Summer and Smoke,* starring the still unknown Geraldine Page. Although off-Broadway had been in existence for a long time, I believe that these two simultaneous successes were really decisive.

One noted a concern for form, a quest for the most varied means of expression in your productions during the early years. . . .

JULIAN: We wanted to go quite far. Yet looking back now, the things we did seem a lot less original than we thought at the time. From the outset, our approach had been defined as "avant-garde" theatre, but our attempts seem rather feeble today. We chose marginal plays that placed their emphasis on language, on a certain fantastic quality.

In spite of everything, we had it in us to bring some real pleasure to a few lovers of the theatre, to a small intellectual community.

You have always designed the sets for your productions. How did you and Judith divide the work during the early years?

JULIAN: I took care of the sets, the costumes, and the administrative work. Occasionally, I directed. Judith's directing, which includes most of the plays, has exceptional precision, in my opinion. I am quite imaginative and have lots of ideas, but I do not have Judith's eye for focusing right on the heart of the matter. That's what makes all the difference!

6

100th STREET
AND BROADWAY

In need of money and working at all kinds of jobs, the Becks were to spend nearly two years looking for a suitable place to reestablish the Living Theatre. When they found one, it was not exactly a theatre. Robert Edmond Jones's advice of long ago had something to do with the choice they made—having closely scrutinized nearly a hundred locations, they settled on a loft in a wood building on the corner of Broadway and 100th Street. The ground floor was occupied by a grocery, the second floor by a Cypriote club, and on top of that was the loft. The rent was ninety dollars a month—five months painfully paid in advance. But they could rehearse and work at last, and the loft quickly became known as "The Studio." There was neither publicity nor ticket sale; a symbolic bread basket was placed at the entrance for voluntary contributions, and the actors shared in the receipts.

The stage was furnished with discarded pieces of furniture and junk, the costumes left over from *Ubu the King* were transformed into curtains, and the seats came from just about everywhere. The cost of setting all this up and of preparing the first production totaled one hundred and thirty-six dollars! Sixty-five seats awaited an audience, and word got around. Friends and friends of friends made their way uptown, and after the fall of 1954 people had to be turned away.

W. H. Auden's *The Age of Anxiety,* a play in verse, was the first production. It had been in rehearsal for over a year, whenever time could be spared, but it failed to win over the audiences. It had a number of memorable features, nevertheless: a twelve-tone musical score by Jackson MacLow, a frequent collaborator, and the appearance of James Agee in the role of a radio announcer.

Strindberg's *The Spook Sonata* followed. As the Becks staged it, the scenery vanished at the end, except for Böcklin's "Isle of the Dead" on the wall at the back of the stage. The sweet-yet-sad music seemed to emanate from the isle in the painting itself; it was composed by Alan Hovhaness, who was to serve as the Living Theatre's music director for years to come—a labor of love, surely, for a composer who has attained success not only on Broadway, for his music to Clifford Odets' *The Flowering Peach,* but for his serious music as well.

Cocteau's *Orpheus* was the successful opener of the 1954-1955 season. It was followed by *The Idiot King,* a gloomy morality play in verse that dealt with pacifism and destiny, the work of the poet and publisher Claude Fredericks. Most spectators were annoyed by it.

Pirandello was particularly suited to a Living Theatre production; the manner in which the company rendered the ambiguity, incommunicability, the hopeless gropings of consciousness and words toward capturing the unconscious in *Tonight We Improvise,* which followed *The Idiot King,* resulted in a remarkable success. The play ran continuously for four months.

Phèdre followed in May, 1955, and was the first English-language performance of the Racine tragedy on a professional stage in New York. It was also the first time the Living Theatre ventured to interpret a classic, all previous productions having depended upon playwrights of the late nineteenth and the twentieth centuries. Richard Edelman, who had directed *The Idiot King,* was invited to direct *Phèdre,* and these were to remain (with the exception of the later collective productions in Europe) the only occasions when an outsider directed a Living Theatre performance. The translation of the play had been done by Judith and Julian.

The Becks remember their approach to Racine as having been "very formal." Julian designed the set and costumes, as always. They were based on a totally white stage, which symbolized the gleaming clear light of the ancient world as it might have been imagined in the seventeenth century. Judith played Phèdre. The reviewers compared the staging to an abstract Japanese ballet. The problems of how to deliver poetry and how to treat verse in acting remained unsolved. Still, the public did not mind; the run of the play had to be extended twice. Judith's first arrest for pacifist activities was during this same period.

In October, Paul Goodman was on the playbill once again. *The Young Disciple,* as is the case with all of Goodman's work, was a shocker; it was an adaptation of the Gospel According to St. Mark and dealt with the problems encountered by youth in quest of higher wisdom. Merce Cunningham did the choreography.

Destiny closed in on the loft in November, 1955, in the shape of the New York City Department of Buildings. It was decreed that the number of seats in the theatre exceeded the limits of safety and had to be reduced to eighteen if the theatre was to remain in the building. Before departing, the company gave a public reading of William Carlos Williams' *Many Loves,* which had been chosen for production but was now to be delayed by circumstance for more than three years.

For Judith and Julian, the loft represented the ideal theatre, sorrowfully missed, up to the time of their great European adventure. There were no tickets and virtually no bought publicity; there was hard work and the spectators either made a contribution or did not make one, though they were more than generous as a rule. In the Becks' view, this state of virtual mendicancy was in effect a thorough rejection of a society where plays were assessed in accordance with their cost of production—"the symptom of a society which builds and judges according to the price and not to the needs." It was for that reason, too, that Julian constructed scenery and costumes out of the most ordinary of materials—strings, rags, rubbish of all types. The Living Theatre used actors who agreed to live in austerity. Stringent economizing was the general rule. When beauty emerged, it emerged out of inventiveness, offering itself as an extra bonus. Sometimes.

7 | A THEATRE FOR DREAMING. . . .

The closing of the loft was discouraging for Judith and Julian, but it did not stop them. They began to look for a new location immediately, having in mind something less susceptible to municipal difficulties but still suited to their needs. Once again, it took them about two years to find and furnish the new home of the Living Theatre. Six years later, in 1963, it was seized by the Internal Revenue Service.

They found the place in June, 1957, signed the lease in October, moved in in November, and started a new drive for funds. It took five months to gain approval from the authorities for their remodeling plans, and seven more to carry them out. They did not employ the services of a contractor; they did everything themselves. A hundred volunteers—actors, painters, dancers, most of them well-known—mixed plaster and wielded trowels and paintbrushes. A distinguished architect stated later that it would have taken professionals ten times longer to achieve lesser results at forty times the cost.

Their new home was situated on the corner of Sixth Avenue and 14th Street. It had once been a department store and had plenty of space, offering numerous architectural possibilities. Julian drew up the plans under the guidance of a good architect, Paul Williams. The ground floor was occupied by stores; the second story housed the theatre with its lobby; the third included dressing rooms for thirty actors, a lecture room, and a rehearsal hall; the fourth afforded space for scenery and costume storage.

The Living Theatre had not created an ordinary theatre. Over the years, Judith and Julian had come to envision the theatre as a sort of dream experienced by the spectator-dreamer, and the building on 14th Street was going to embody this conception. In order to make the spectator feel that he was passing from one level to another, "(. . .) the lobby was painted (. . .) brightly, the brick walls exposed, like the walls of a courtyard, the ceiling painted sky blue, a fountain running as in a public square, and kiosks, one for coffee and one for books, standing in the center. The lobby was the day room; the theatre was painted black, narrower and narrower stripes converging towards the stage, concentrating the focus, as if one were inside an old fashioned Kodak, looking out thru the lens, the eye of the dreamer in the dark room, the seats painted in hazy gray, lavender, and sand, with oversize circus numbers on them in bright orange, lemon and magenta, all this Williams' attempt to aid us to achieve an atmosphere for the dreamers and their waking up when they walked out into the lobby."[1]

The lobby was a large, irregularly shaped room where one could stroll about, sit on benches, and chat with the actors during intermissions. The enameled doors were the work of Paul Hultberg, and David Weinrib sculpted the fountain. The theatre itself had neither wings nor defined boundaries for the stage, except for an important space for sets on one side; the audience was virtually engulfing the stage.

From this time on, Judith and Julian lived solely for the theatre. They gave up all the numerous pursuits they had been engaged in during previous years. Their time was now spent on rehearsals, on fund raising—their perpetual *leitmotif*. They always found time to participate in pacifist demonstrations, and they were arrested about six times in all before 1963. During the hiatus between the closing of the loft and the opening on 14th Street they were ar-

---

[1] Julian Beck in Kenneth H. Brown, *op. cit.*

rested for participating in demonstrations against civil defense exercises, which signified to them the United States' commitment to nuclear armament and the admission of the possibility of nuclear attack and counterattack. Twenty-eight persons were arrested during the first such demonstration in New York; five years later there were five hundred demonstrators; the following year, five thousand; the year after that, the exercises were abandoned. Non-violence had won a battle.

8 | THE BLACK SPOT

You remarked in reference to the Federal Theatre that at all costs one must avoid simplification with the pretext of making the spectator's work easier for him. At the opposite pole, your European productions—and I presume most of your American ones as well—have been largely obscure, in that they require knowledge of certain points of reference that the uninformed spectator does not possess. Do you think that it is possible to grasp the essentials without a solid cultural grounding?

JULIAN: This may be somewhat "mystical" on my part, but I believe that even if the audience does not consciously comprehend what one sometimes calls the "symbolism" in our plays, it will nevertheless register in their unconscious. When something that is clearly understood penetrates the brain, say, "The state is a bad thing," it will leave a little spot, to put it graphically. But when something that is not understood penetrates, everything will be black, and the brain must then dispel the blackness. It is like a dream, whether good or bad, that is capable of haunting the dreamer for years. When the spectator is confronted by certain images, he may leave the theatre without having really grasped their meaning, yet they may well affect his future actions. It is imperative to unsettle people, to offer them disturbing images. Their effects may be altogether beneficial, carrying over into everyday life, which is the idea, after all. . . . Then again, sometimes we may offer images that are so simple that they are not accepted. . . .

9 | 14th STREET

Judith and Julian presented nine productions, comprised of ten plays, between January, 1959, and October, 1963. They revived the Monday night gatherings where plays were read—for example, in 1960 they did public readings covering all the Greek tragic poets—poetry was recited, concerts and "happenings" were given. Also, they opened a studio of dramatic arts in the building in the spring of 1959.

At first the Living Theatre was operated as a regular corporation, with stockholders. At the end of the first year, Julian realized it was not possible to promise stockholders any return on their investment. During the loft period, the Becks functioned as an unincorporated business; on 14th Street they organized a corporation again, with a limited number of members. Money had always been and was to remain the most agonizing problem to the Becks. True anarchists that they are, they found it impossible to accept most methods of commercial transactions. They maintain that "the entire economy is strangling most of the creative efforts of all men, farmers, workers, scientists, whoever, all achieve whatever they achieve in spite of the structures of Mammon, and not because of them. Then the work you do in the theatre becomes in all its parts an attempt to get men to do away with the whole system. One of the lessons. But Mammon does not disintegrate just because a theatre seating 162 people happens to say so. He has his revenge. With us it was continual. If we were always working for his withering away, he never removed from us the yoke."[1]

[1] Julian Beck, "How to Close a Theatre," *op. cit.*

They were fighting *for* money *against* money. How could they do otherwise? Their radicalism had not yet reached its peak, however. In 1963, immediately after the forced closing of the 14th Street theatre, Julian declared to the press that he was formulating a plan to perform in public places, in the streets. In 1968 this plan was to become even closer to his heart.

The 14th Street theatre opened with William Carlos Williams' *Many Loves.* Composed of three distinct sections, each with its own characters, the play is unified by the theme of love. In counterpoint to the three prose sections runs a connective text in free verse. It describes the complex relationship between a young man, who is the author of the three prose sections, and an older man whom he once loved, who loves him still, and who might become the producer of the play. The young man is in love with the leading lady—played by Judith—in the three prose sections, and he is constrained to conceal his love until almost the end. The older man senses what is happening and takes matters in hand, being the strongest of the three. He eventually accepts his failure to recapture the author's love and arranges his marriage to the leading lady, even to the point of sending out the invitations. During all of this, he freely criticizes the play itself. Some people have seen in it a struggle between art (author and actors) and the jealousy of the world (the older man) in the play.

The public gave it a warm reception, and its Pirandellian aspect charmed European audiences as well during the 1961 tour. While the spectators are taking their seats, electricians and actors bustle about on the empty stage. There is a cry, "A fuse is blown!" and the lights, which have been off, go on and the play begins. Julian directed *Many Loves*[2] and

----

[2] Julian also directed: *Beyond the Mountains, Tonight We Improvise, The Cave at Machpelah, Women*

the Becks' son, Garry, played the role of a five-year-old child in the play.

Paul Goodman's *The Cave at Machpelah,* a play in verse, followed in June, 1959. It chronicled the story of Abraham and his family, and the public was bored. It became the biggest flop in the history of the Living Theatre: it ran for seven performances. The problems posed by acting a verse play imposed themselves on the production once again with fatal results. The failure of the play was all the more distressing because it was to be offered in repertory with *Many Loves*—for the first time in years the Becks had come close to reviving the cherished repertory goal.

Meanwhile, the Becks were awarded the Lola d'Annunzio Prize—a sort of off-Broadway equivalent of the Antoinette Perry Awards. And two weeks after the closing of *The Cave at Machpelah* a new play, the first work of a twenty-eight-year-old Chicago playwright, Jack Gelber, was unveiled—*The Connection.* The play caused a great deal of attention, and the repertory system of the Living Theatre was to be successfully maintained from the opening of *The Connection* until the end of the theatre's American period.

---

of *Trachis, Man Is Man.* Judith directed all the others, except *Phèdre* and *The Idiot King,* which were directed by Richard Edelman.

10 THE CONNECTION

The Pirandellian identity of theatre and life—displayed in other tonalities in the Living Theatre's repertory on earlier occasions—was the key to Judith's direction of *The Connection*. Gelber had brought the play to the Becks himself, in 1958. "He couldn't afford postage," Julian recalls. "I read some passages at random as I always do, then took it to Judith's room and told her that I thought we had to do it. It's a funny thing, but *The Connection* and *The Brig* were the two plays that made a splash, and we decided to do them both the very day we received each of the scripts."

In the vernacular of drug addicts, "connection" means a person who sells drugs. The play deals with a group of addicts waiting in the apartment of one of them to make a connection with "Cowboy," a Negro pusher. It is not presented as a staged performance but as a "real" gathering of "real" addicts, as conceived by a movie producer who is there with his crew and who speaks to the audience. Among the addicts, who act as addicts do while waiting for their fix, are four jazz musicians who improvise on their instruments from time to time. The "author" of the film script, who is seated in the audience, protests the changes the actors are making in his scenario. At last Cowboy arrives, accompanied by a Salvation Army Sister he met in the streets where police were patrolling. One of the addicts knowingly takes a larger dose than he ought to, and collapses. He recovers. Immediately after this dramatic incident, the author realizes that the action on the stage has completely got out from under his control.

For Judith, the play moves like a pendulum between two liberating forces—jazz and drugs. In effect, it was conceived as sequences of monologues and scraps of jazz, and Shirley Clarke's film version blundered in superimposing the text on the music, which device erased a very precise structure. The music, after all, was not meant to be accompaniment but one of the polarities. Although jazz men are often on drugs, jazz is at once a result of the drug and a superior—or another—drug. The "Connection" is anything that creates contact. The connection linking the actors or addicts is unlike that linking the musicians, because the latter have a means of self-expression. When the addicts are not merely addicts but attempt to talk to each other, when the jazz musicians try to communicate by means of words, they all leave their own worlds and enter a sort of desperate no man's land.

There is contact, roughly structured, between the actors and the musicians, between the audience and the actors, and so on. The current passes on. Judith and Julian hung a naked bulb on a long wire over center stage; it was not just a prop to them but another symbol of "connection." Connection is energy and interchange, at times destructive: the addicts are destroyed by the musicians in the play. At times—even often—connection is creative, generative: early in the play someone inserts the male plug of a phonograph into a female one, and it plays a record of the late Charlie Parker—the great jazz man is being electrically resuscitated, as it were. The work of the musician thus lives on, soon to be outdone by real life, to be sure, by the music improvised on stage by the four musicians; still, the impetus had come from Charlie Parker. This is also to be compared with what is said later on concerning Antigone's gesture of gathering the dust.

Looking at it in terms of the acting style, this is

a significant occurrence. The musicians, being necessarily "real," don't mind the public, and their relationship to the audience is entirely different from that of actors. Actors interpret roles—contrary to the belief expressed by many, the actors did not carry their roles as addicts into their private lives; some of them have never had any experiences with drugs—whereas musicians "play" themselves with considerable freedom. Judith was quick to point out the advantages of this type of self representation: "When a jazz musician plays his music, he enters into *personal* contact with the public; when he goes home after he has played, one who talks to him knows that there is no difference between the way he is now and the way he was on the stage. This type of relationship with the audience creates in him a great relaxation. *The Connection* represented a very important advance for us in this respect: from then on, the actors began *to play themselves.*"

The direction taken by the actors, which combined real and sham improvisation, disoriented the audiences; at times they were taken in completely. During the three-year run of the play, a total of about fifty spectators fainted when Leach sticks a hypodermic in his arm. Audiences invariably applauded the actor who was presented to them at the beginning of the play as "Jaybird, the author of *The Connection.*" In the same vein, make-believe and reality were deliberately blended by Judith during intermission, when the actors mingled with the audience, asking for a fix in the characteristic tone and manner of addicts.

Plays had been written about drug addiction before *The Connection,* but they skimmed the surface only—Michael Gazzo's *A Hatful of Rain,* for example. None made a frontal attack on the subject, and none abstained from expressing judgments when the right moment came along. In stark contrast, *The Connection* offered neither a solution nor moral reflections—nor a defense, for that matter. What it offered was at best an opportunity to make relative comparisons: What are narcotics if not simply another form of alienation? They may be more harmful to the body, but are they more harmful to the spirit, to personal morality? Is alienation brought on by work or money more acceptable, less pernicious?

Judith and Julian saw no deception in the artifice of presenting a theatrical event as if it were real, because even when a play obtrudes very hard— as it often does with Pirandello, for example—the spectator always has his own points of reference to hold on to. Nevertheless, the uncompromising honesty that characterizes Judith and Julian must have been affected by this practice after a while. (In *The Brig* [see page 63] the "deception" was on a much lesser scale, and in the European productions the direct commitment of the actors was accented as much as possible.)

During this phase of their work, the Becks were already stating the basic reality of the actor's and the spectator's true identity. As a matter of course, the actor has a privileged status on the stage, as he has in life. In his roles, he speaks in the third person; he speaks for others, for his roles. Meanwhile, the spectator's tendency is to rid himself of disturbing questions that may be aroused by certain plays; this is theatre, these are actors, this is a play, he tells himself. Consequently, he does not *really* feel; he experiences mentally. In order to make him feel, his physical being must be struck.

Pirandello would remain in the background. The Living Theatre was to choose the way of Antonin Artaud, who regarded the obstinate adherence to rational means in fighting barbarism and "evil" as the major flaw of Western culture.

11 | ARTAUD? STRAIGHT AHEAD. . . .

In effect, the supernaturalism of *The Connection* had nothing in common with Artaud's "theatre of cruelty." In one important respect, the troupe's productions have conformed to Artaud's theories —even though the Becks were unacquainted with these theories until some years later—that is, in their concern with involving the audience in the adventure of the stage. The Living Theatre emphasized concepts that unify and integrate and articulate. Can one call it a "poetic" theatre? For Judith and Julian, it was a theatre that demonstrated the fact that we live on various and diverse levels and that everyday language, pragmatic and materialistic, was inadequate for conveying such variousness and diversity. This was the source of their respect for the word during the early years, for the chosen word, the true word, the honest word. "The word must join us, else it is just another barricade," Julian wrote. "We kill one another when we do not speak the truth, it is the way to early death. But when you speak to me true I live, and you, a little longer. It is our joint struggle against death."[1]

Poetic theatre, formal research, honesty. . . . *The Connection* spoke the true word through fiction, a fact that troubled the Becks to some extent. How to convey directly the solitude of the addict, how to relate his flight from reality—if it is one—to other, more "respectable" forms of flight? How to perform a play in which, perhaps for the first time, the color

[1] Julian Beck in Kenneth H. Brown, *op. cit.*

of skin means nothing? How to make the physical torment of an overdose palpable to the spectator?

For the Living Theatre, this meant making common cause with the thesis that addicts were worthy of interest and respect and that they were but victims of a system that destroys the individual with a pernicious subtlety—that system being Western civilization. In the program, Judith Malina dedicated her work to the memory of Thelma Gadsen, "dead of an overdose of heroin (. . .) and to all the junkies dead or alive in the Women's House of Detention." It was in both these senses that one understood the meaning of the troupe's "commitment" in performing a play such as *The Connection.*

There was no feeling, in the Living Theatre's production of this Jack Gelber play, of moving in the direction charted by Artaud; that was not to come until several years later with *The Brig.* Be that as it may, the encounter could not help but come about. Not resting content with merely performing, being intent on playing on the spectator's nerves as well as on his mind, these were signs of a spontaneous move toward Artaud.

A sizable obstacle stood in the way: Artaud was not yet translated into English. During the summer of 1958, at the time the troupe was moving into the 14th Street building, Mary Caroline Richards sent the Becks the manuscript of her translation of *The Theatre and Its Double,* which was to be published by Grove Press. It was a revelation to the Becks. Were they not also yearning to return to a less adulterated way of living and feeling? Had they not also frequently turned their attention to the Oriental forms of theatre and the authors whom that form venerates? Artaud would undoubtedly endorse Julian's words:

". . . in the process of protecting ourselves from the barbaric instincts and acts we feared, we simultaneously cut ourselves off

from all impulsive sensation and made ourselves the heartless monsters that wage
wars, that burn and gas (. . .) that enslave
the blacks, plan bacteriological weapons,
annihilate Carthage and Hiroshima, humili-
ate and crush, conduct inquisitions, hang
men in cages to die of starvation (. . .),
wipe out the Indians, the buffalo, exploit
the peon, lock men in prisons away from
natural sex, invent the gallows, the garrotte,
the block, the guillotine, the electric chair,
the gas chamber, the firing squad, that take
young men in their prime and deliberately
teach them to kill, I mean we actually teach
people to kill, and that go about our daily
business while one person every six seconds
dies of starvation."[2]

Artaud wanted to put an end to theatre that
was mere play-acting without consequences, as it
were. The theatre existed "to drain abscesses collectively," like the plague, to reveal vileness, hypocrisy,
illusion. Hence, it had to become the "time of evil."
The stage must not remain a place where texts are
recited but be "a concrete physical place which asks
to be filled, and to be given its own concrete language to speak," a language "intended for the senses
and independent of speech." Inasmuch as Western
theatre is what it is and fails to separate itself "from
the idea of a *performed text*," it must enroll in the
school of Oriental theatre, which is "pre-logical."
There, sounds and movements have an ideographic
content, much superior to European pantomime that
is the *genre* most comparable to it; but whereas

[2] Julian Beck in Kenneth H. Brown, *op. cit.* Com-
pare with: "We are still living under the rule of logic,
that is what I wanted to say. But the logical proceedings
of our days only still apply to the resolution of problems
of secondary interest." (Translated from: André Breton,
Manifeste du surréalisme, 1924.)

pantomime can represent only words, Oriental theatre can express "ideas, attitudes of mind, aspects of nature." Noises, screams, vibrations surround the spectators. The catharsis, which must be successful, leads the spectator to denounce the world and to perceive that "our present social state is iniquitous and should be destroyed."

A theatre of awakening, then, for disaster is imminent. The spectator shall be "engulfed and physically affected" by the performance that places him at the very heart of the action. This theatre of "cruelty"—the term not to be taken as one signifying sadistic perversion but in the sense of "an appetite for life, a cosmic rigor and implacable necessity" —will be exceedingly, even extra-sensory-lucid, one of "implacable intention and decision, irreversible and absolute determination." It will be quite the opposite of Western theatre, which has decided in favor of presenting us with inert ideas, "unable to stir up in their course a whole system of natural analogies as in Oriental languages."

As it turned out, the Living Theatre was to stay content to follow its natural inclinations and to make do without Artaud, although the discovery of Artaud's work was an invaluable stimulus, confirmation, and encouragement to them. The avant-gardism of the early years had been relatively rational. Artaud had held out the invitation to the journey: there were territories still undiscovered, there were visions beyond controlled perception.

GAMES OF CHANCE

It cost nine hundred dollars to mount *The Connection,* and the reviews in the dailies were terrible. Fortunately, it was possible to alternate subsequent performances in repertory with *Many Loves* and keep the play on the boards until the weeklies reviewed it. Their reviews were excellent, and two-and-a-half years later the troupe celebrated the 700th performance of *The Connection.*

At the time the Gelber play embarked on its remarkable run all members of the troupe were drawing a weekly salary of forty-five dollars. Twelve actors—half of the company—had been with Judith and Julian for three years, and two of those actors dated back to the Cherry Lane period of 1951-1952.

Encouraged by the success of *The Connection,* the Becks reinstated Pirandello's *Tonight We Improvise* in the repertory. It had had an excellent reception four and a half years earlier on 100th Street. Joseph Shipley wrote that it was "the best performance of a Pirandello play in New York in over twenty years."

There were no new productions until June, 1960. The repertory consisted of *The Connection, Tonight We Improvise,* and *Many Loves.* Recognition came in the form of an award from the Newspaper Guild, and three "Obies" from the *Village Voice* for the best direction of the year, best new play of the year, and, for Warren Finnerty's work in *The Connection,* best performance of the year.

On June 22, 1960, two new plays, Jackson MacLow's *The Marrying Maiden* and Sophocles' *Women of Trachis,* were presented under the title,

"The Theatre of Chance." They were experimental productions, inspired by the theories of the composer John Cage, and they remained in repertory for nearly a year.

The MacLow play was the more interesting one from the group's point of view—opportunities for improvisation were far greater in this play than in *The Connection,* which had only a few spots that allowed for uncharted stage business and improvised dialogue. *The Marrying Maiden* turned out to be almost entirely different from one performance to the next. The author, drawing on the rules of chance of the hexagrams in the *I Ching,* constructed six dialogue-and-character scenes. He provided a series of directions for the actors consisting of five degrees of vocal volume and five degrees of tempo in delivery And, he specified, by means of a hundred adverbs and adverbial phrases, the tone in which certain words or groups of words were to be spoken—with gaiety, sorrow, and other emotions following each other solely by chance.

Judith Malina wanted to go even further. She prepared cards of the texts provided by the author for each scene. She then created a special part—a dice thrower, played by Henry Proach—and it was his throw of the dice that determined the sequence in which actors, or John Cage's taped "music," were to be used. Each time Proach threw a seven, he handed a random action card to an actor, who then performed it. Each time he threw a five the tape recorder was activated—Cage's "music" actually consisted of a taped reading of the play, with certain parts electronically distorted by Cage but most of the text remaining audible.

Sophocles' *Women of Trachis,* in the Ezra Pound adaptation the Becks used, relates the death of Heracles, not by the weapon of an enemy but by the unwitting hand of his own loving wife, who had been attempting to regain his love by means of a love potion. The role of fate (i.e., chance) in this well-known myth linked it organically to *The Marrying Maiden,* hence the production title "The Theatre of Chance."

In November, 1960, the Living Theatre gave its 1000th performance. A sponsoring committee was formed and included such prominent people as John Cage, Jean Cocteau, Merce Cunningham, Elaine and Willem de Kooning, Allen Ginsberg, Frederick Kiesler, William Baziotes, Paul Goodman, Tennessee Williams, William Carlos Williams, and Shelley Winters.

In December, Brecht's *In the Jungle of the Cities* was introduced. Brecht's son, Stefan, who holds the American rights to his father's plays, had seen and liked *Tonight We Improvise* and *The Connection* and suggested to the Becks that they produce this early play by his father. The play was completed in 1922, before Brecht studied Marxism. It is set in Chicago, from 1912 to 1915. A rich Malayan wood merchant, who has also made a fortune in other, shady, enterprises, voluntarily impoverishes himself to benefit a poor man, Garga. As Garga becomes more powerful he becomes harsh and merciless, while the Malayan adapts himself to poverty and acquires a certain wisdom—an element stressed in this production.

It is clear from the play that the poor and the outcasts had already engaged Brecht's compassion in 1922. The play bears the marks of perhaps too subjective personal memories, and for that reason, possibly, a number of critics have found it obscure. Brecht had been influenced by reading Rimbaud, by a book about Chicago he'd come upon, and by the joy of the Luna Park in Augsburg. The Living Theatre felt the importance of the contribution of Rimbaud as well as of the great Brechtian theme of the corruptive power of money.

Brecht had been virtually unknown in the United States—except for the celebrated Charles Laughton *Galileo* that played in Hollywood and

New York in 1947, after a year's preparation. To be sure, *The Threepenny Opera* enjoyed great popularity, but chiefly because of its resemblance to musical comedy. Prior to 1956, *The Good Woman of Setzuan* and *The Caucasian Chalk Circle* were staged perhaps a dozen times in all, but always outside the mainstream of American theatre, by college or regional players. Thus, the Living Theatre's productions of *In the Jungle of the Cities,* and of *Man Is Man* two years later, were significant theatrical events.

Although the Becks had not seen at that time the Berliner Ensemble, their productions of Brecht's plays were going in a parallel direction—both were grounded in Brecht's theoretical works. Judith's direction of *Jungle* had a great deal of humor; she tried to recapture the spirit of a twenty-four-year-old Brecht who had little respect for established values. Julian imbued his direction of *Man Is Man* with a ferocious spirit. The play was written in 1924, and its protagonist is a longshoreman who puts on the uniform of a soldier friend, finds himself accused of plundering, and is unable to regain his own identity. Julian's direction made it clear that the longshoreman is perfectly aware of his mistakes; he explains them to the audience, rejoins the action, and in the end becomes a mercenary, ready to fight for any cause. Both *Man Is Man* and *Jungle* were very successful productions.

At the end of 1960, the French extended an official invitation to the Living Theatre to appear at the Théâtre des Nations during the following year. Immediately afterward, other unsolicited invitations arrived from Europe, and the Living Theatre was to become the first off-Broadway company to go on a European tour.

Needless to say, money had to be raised for the tour. The State Department declined to underwrite the cost; not long before, a tour by Helen Hayes and her troupe had cost the U.S. one million dollars.

Moreover, Brecht, Gelber, and William Carlos Williams were stronger stuff than *The Glass Menagerie* and *The Miracle Worker* presented by the Helen Hayes troupe. Obviously, the Living Theatre had to organize a private tour, and the winter was spent in raising funds. With $46,000 in hand, an auction was held. Artists and writers, including Willem de Kooning, Robert Rauschenberg, Paul Goodman, and Allen Ginsberg, offered paintings and manuscripts for sale, and the proceeds went toward underwriting the tour. Sixty-one artists and writers contributed works and $25,000 was raised. (According to Julian's approximation, from the time of its founding to 1963 the Living Theatre received $50,000 from subscribers, $75,000 from three private donors, $35,000 in loans, various donations in the sum of $10,000, and the proceeds of the auction. About half of the total of $200,000 was spent on financing the European tours of 1961 and 1962.)

Much to its surprise, the company was extremely well received in Europe. The critics were disagreeable, but the audiences were most enthusiastic. While performing in Berlin, it was learned that the Living Theatre was to be awarded the Grand Prize for Experiment—never before given to an American theatre group—by the Théâtre des Nations and also the prize of the Université du Théâtre des Nations, awarded by its students, and the Drama Critics Medal. Invitations arrived from Greece, Scotland, and Holland. Short of money and time, the company limited its 1961 appearances to Rome, Turin, Milan, Paris, and Frankfurt, and agreements were made to play Paris, Milan, Holland, Poland, Greece, Belgium, Germany, Israel, Turkey, and Britain the following year. But the company was only to appear in Paris, Zurich, Dusseldorf, six towns in Holland, Antwerp, and Brussels in 1962.

Jack Gelber's second play, *The Apple,* was presented in December, 1961, between the two Brecht plays. At that time "the apple" was a term for New York City used by few people outside the world of jazz musicians. In the play Gelber affirms once again—although with less exuberance than in *The Connection*—that the theatre and life are one and the same. The actors are seen serving themselves coffee at a counter on stage. Pretended improvisation dominates and conversation eases at every turn. The talk is of politics, mysticism, social problems; clichés, jokes, and parodies are bandied about. Julian played one of the roles, which could not be characterized as a leading one because none was. There was little explicit action on stage. The actors wore masks depicting insects and animals, according to the author's instructions.

A mannequin with mobile legs and arms is one of the lesser surprises to the audience in this Gelber play. Firecrackers go off under the seats of spectators, a picture created on stage by an "action painter" is put on sale, along with coffee, a "paranoiac Fascist drunk" leaves his seat in the audience, climbs up on stage, and completely unsettles the harmonious atmosphere structured by the actors. Tension begins to build. A yellow skinned actress pleads for a "yellow world" and she is countered not by a white opponent but by a black one who pleads for a "black world," showing up the absurdity of the first plea by offering the alternative of the second. At the heart of the debate, of the play itself, is our culture, our way of life. What will tomorrow be made of? The play has its defects, as plays written for a specific company sometimes do, but at least it has the incidental virtue of posing some important questions.

13

MONEY, MONEY, MONEY

The Apple was the 28th play done by the Living Theatre. Only one more play, *The Brig*, was performed before the exile to Europe. The last years in New York were a constant struggle with financial problems. Julian was to remark in 1964 that he was spending eighty-five per cent of his time on raising money. Creditors were calling without a let-up. The overhead on 14th Street was $3,300 per week, but the capacity gross of $3,800 was rarely attained. The annual deficit was around $25,000. Lack of funds forced a rise in ticket prices, with a five-dollar top in effect on weekends. As workers and students could not afford these prices, the troupe found itself playing to predominantly middle-class audiences, which was quite contrary to its objectives.

Subscribers did what they could, but they could not do everything; one hundred and fifty out of a total of five hundred were contributing more than the fifteen-dollar minimum. Judith and Julian, having neither a secretary nor an accountant, were spending sleepless nights over bookkeeping accounts.

In 1962, with *Man Is Man* running, the Becks were compelled once again to abandon the repertory system. *Man Is Man* called for too many actors to be performed alternately with others requiring smaller casts; publicity cost more if the program changed every night. One attempt at repertory was made during that winter. *The Connection* was to be revived to alternate with *Man Is Man*, but the newspaper strike forced the cancellation of the plan. Thus, *Man Is Man* had a run of 170 performances.

Aspiring to a moneyless society, the Becks nevertheless faced financial problems every single day. The pressure was more acute during the last New York years than ever before.

During several preceding years the Living Theatre had paid nearly $20,000 a year in taxes. In 1963, it no longer could. According to custom the Becks turned to the big foundations, even though they suspected their well-known anarchist beliefs would not help their chances for a grant. The Ford Foundation refused to grant the Living Theatre a penny, on the grounds that the company was not paying its actors adequately enough to guarantee a degree of professionalism. This, in spite of the fact that the Living Theatre was awarded three prizes by the Théâtre des Nations, and that its actors regularly won the annual "best off-Broadway performance of the year" awards of the *Village Voice*. Judith and Julian concluded that the Ford Foundation judged actors on the basis of salary! Then a foundation representative pointed out that even if the company played consistently to capacity houses, it could still not pay its actors suitably. It was clear to the Becks that the Ford Foundation was out to prove that art could finance itself from an initial capital, and that it wanted to see "a chain of Ford Theatres across America," with comfortable budgets and a sound business outlook. Of course, this required the production of shows that the public would "want to support"—congenial, uncontroversial things.

As for the Rockefeller Foundation, Judith and Julian were invited to a sumptuous lunch. John D. Rockefeller III was there himself. The theatre's books were examined at great length, and foundation officials spent a delightful afternoon at the theatre. Later, when their financial plight was the most acute it had ever been, Julian telephoned the foundation. He was told cordially that there had been no plan at any time to give the Living Theatre a grant. The intentions of the foundation had been limited to establishing a study which would then serve as a model for other foundations that wished to support the performing arts. Judith was later to immortalize the meeting with John D. the Third in a little poem of vengeance, "On the Day of the Death of Pope John XXIII," published in the August, 1964, issue of *Fuck You,* a magazine edited by Ed Sanders.

Faithful friends helped the company whenever they could. But the day was to come when they would no longer be able to save it.

In 1961, the Living Theatre obtained the designation "educational institution," which might have made it eligible for tax exemption. However, the law firm that would have seen the matter through wanted a fifteen-hundred-dollar retainer. It proved to be impossible to raise the money for that purpose; whenever an equivalent sum happened to be available, there were always other, more urgent needs to be met. . . .

14

THE BRIG

The premiere of Kenneth Brown's *The Brig* took place on May 15th, 1963. It was certainly the most dazzling act of rebellion against Establishment theatre to have found expression in the history of the Living Theatre. *The Brig* represented civil disobedience, and could not even be properly called a play; essentially, it was but another manifestation of the spirit of the World Wide General Strike for Peace, which the Becks had organized one week before the premiere. They had closed the theatre, and their call for strike had succeeded in paralyzing a number of schools and various other activities in many countries throughout the world, even if it had not attracted as many sympathizers as they had hoped.

During their 1961 tour of Europe, the Becks obtained the *"Modellbuch"* of Brecht's *Antigone,* and when they eventually produced it, six years later, the production stressed the play's pacifist values. By the same token, after their return from the 1962 European tour, they felt the time had come once again for them to join work and anarchist convictions into a single act. That is how the strike call and *The Brig* came about.

Gertrude Stein's *Doctor Faustus Lights the Lights* was a representation of hell in the form of the theatre of ideas, as the Becks had presented it twelve years earlier. *The Brig* depicted the very plunge into hell that was but glimpsed at in the Stein play.

Kenneth H. Brown was born in Brooklyn in 1936. He attended a Jesuit high school, served in the

Marine Corps, studied briefly at Columbia, became a bartender. When he came to write *The Brig* he could not quite decide how to define it, for it was not theatre in the traditional sense, lacking such criteria as temporal progression and structured plot. In the end, he called it *The Brig: A Concept for Theater or Film.*

In its original usage, "brig" meant the place of confinement for offenders on United States men-of-war; today the term covers Navy and Marine prisons in general. When Brown was assigned to a Marine base in the Far East the brig was a wood barracks, painted green, approximately one hundred and thirty feet long and fifty-four feet wide, situated in the center of the camp. On one side it had a roofless section topped by barbed wire.

The brig contained individual cells and a dormitory with thirty bunk beds enclosed by iron grating. A corridor led to the back of the building, which accommodated showers, a guards' office, and, next to the door referred to as "the door to freedom," a blackboard listing the offenses committed by each prisoner.

The Marines use depersonalization as the method of "rehabilitating" those who have committed infractions. The prisoners' heads are shaved and they are forbidden to speak to each other. They must address the guards in a loud, clear, impersonal tone of voice, always in the same manner: "Sir, prisoner number . . . requests permission to speak, Sir." The limitation of speech, the all too tenuous link in drawing people close to one another, serves to isolate them irremediably. In one sense the brig symbolizes a world dominated by money and power, a world doomed, in the Living Theatre's belief, unless man takes action.

The floor is sectioned off by a dozen painted white lines, and every time a prisoner wants to move from one section to another he must request permission to cross the imaginary barrier. A mistake is punished by blows in the stomach and various other humiliations.

All moves must be executed at a running pace, or, if that is physically impossible, at a trot—never walking. The guards' manner alternates between cynicism, sarcasm, and fervent conviction, depending on the situation. They choose the insults most likely to really hurt. One of the more subtle torments they practice is the "search." There are two varieties. In the first, upon a guard's command, "Break down for a frisk!" the prisoner unties his shoelaces, unbuttons his buttons, and grabs the iron grating with both hands. In the second, the guard barks out, "Break down for a shakedown!" whereupon the prisoner removes his clothes, except for underwear and socks, places them in a pile on the floor, and hands them over piece by piece for inspection.

Brown's script is very short, no more than about forty pages. Six scenes, covering a single day in a brig on Okinawa from reveille to bedtime, are divided into two acts. The eleven prisoners are drawn from various social strata, and represent a cross-section of society.

Act I opens with the intimidation of a new arrival as he is awakened by a guard. General reveille. A big rush to wash up. Perfunctory gymnastics in the open area. "You touched me, you lousy insect," a guard shouts at a prisoner. "You actually came in contact with my clothing, infesting it with the disease of your stinking self!" The prisoner is punched in the stomach.

The morning cigarette. Inhaling and exhaling are executed in rhythm on command. Cigarettes are taken from the mouths of those who did not rise fast enough at reveille or otherwise displeased the guards during the morning.

General search. A bullied prisoner breaks into tears. He is not tough enough, and will be transferred out of the Marine Corps. Having put on a rain hat without a reason, a prisoner is ordered to recite his transgression to a toilet seat at the top of his voice.

Act II opens on a feverish clean-up. The reward for good work during the clean-up is half an hour off to write a letter. The Marine Hymn is sung. A prisoner who has spent sixteen years in the Corps collapses with a nervous breakdown. He is removed. Another is freed for good conduct. A new one arrives. He is told that he may speak to another prisoner for the first and last time.

Showers, bed. "Are all my children asleep?" a guard shouts out. "Yes, Sir!" the reply comes resoundingly and immediately.

In her preparations for staging the play, Judith decided that the only effective way to proceed was to get right to the heart of the matter. Consequently, she began by reproducing the abnormal relationships of the brig among the members of the cast itself. The company submitted to the experiment voluntarily, even though it proved to be the most trying one imaginable for actors used to working in the least formal of circumstances. Judith drew up a list of regulations and the company voted unanimously to abide by it:

Rehearsal Discipline Rules:

a. Actors will sign in before Rehearsal Time is called. Actors should arrive five minutes prior to called time, in the auditorium, to be ready for places when called.

b. During Rehearsal Time, actors who are not on stage will remain in the auditorium, ready to be called unless specifically dismissed by the stage manager.

c. During Rehearsal Time, there is to be no business or discussion other than that relating to the rehearsal.

d. No eating during Rehearsal Time.

e. Actors not required on stage may smoke in the first rows of the auditorium, where

ash trays will be provided. No smoking in
other parts of the auditorium. Backstage
rules will be posted by the stage manager.

These rules were supplemented by other enjoin-
ders, such as the prohibition against any kind of
dress other than what was to be worn in the play—
T-shirts and baggy pants for the prisoners, khaki
uniforms for the guards—against jewelry and other
decorative items, and against chatting and small
talk. Tardiness, unexcused absence, causing delays,
uncooperativeness, refusal to allow costume inspection, damaging one's costume (actors were responsible for their costumes down to the last button), all
these incurred the penalty of having to perform
chores that heretofore had been shared by members
of the company and were now meted out as a matter
of punishment.

A system of "cry for mercy" was instituted,
according to which any actor who felt that he was
about to crack could ask for a five-minute break at
any time. (This dispensation was to be utilized quite
often.) A diabolical technique was being employed
in the preparation of the play; in Judith's metaphor
it was not unlike the act of inoculating oneself with
a deadly virus. The atmosphere of the rehearsals became charged with hostility. A terrible solitude over-
came the actors who, for artistic ends, accepted the
constraints of the "brig." Making an allusion to Artaud, Judith Malina compared them to people who
would meet the Red Death in their own fortified
palace. The brig had become a reality that was being
tested by the actors, day after day. Their behavior
was becoming the behavior of victims and tormen-
tors. They felt the world was hemming them in from
all sides, and they felt ill protected.

The success of the production would depend on
the accuracy of representation. Judith did not want
to substitute; she wanted the actors to experience
directly. By this means too, the public would be able

to feel immediately and directly the horror of the brig. The idea originated with Artaud, and this was the first occasion when the Living Theatre deliberately used the inspiration they had drawn from his theories. "Artaud believed," wrote Julian, "that if we could only be made to feel, really feel anything, then we might find all this suffering intolerable, the pain too great to bear, we might put an end to it, and then being able to feel we might truly feel the joy, the joy of everything else, of loving, of creating, of being at peace, and of being ourselves."[1]

Life is not unyielding, rigid; only death is. Everything that restricts and constrains is "infernal," and so is any structure that overlooks the supple flexibility of life, of spirit, of body. One finds the idea developed again in *Mysteries*. The brig is the paradigm of such structures. For Judith and Julian, the brig was the image of the world as a whole and, by analogy, of such microcosms as the school, the family, the factory, the state—of all human associations not based on anarchist principles.

Judith and Julian believed in non-violence before they became anarchists. To change the world? "Yes!" By war and force? "No!" Revolution is desirable, provided it does not jeopardize human lives. Force is always to be condemned, whatever its motives, be they those of the Russian Revolution, anarchists who plant bombs and assassinate, existing Communist regimes based on oppression, or all armed forces everywhere. The Becks want to unify and harmonize at all levels of human life, but *not at any price*. They want to unify, to integrate man, body and soul, because "civilized" man is man divided before he is anything else; he is also a monster "whose faculty of deriving thoughts from acts, instead of identifying acts with thoughts, is developed to an absurdity" (Artaud). Non-violence and anti-militarism are not sufficient for Judith and Julian.

[1] Julian Beck in Kenneth H. Brown, *op. cit.*

They have adopted the most specific of anarchist tenets: suppression of the state, of all forms of authority (politics, education, bourgeois morality), of monetary transactions; creation of groupings that are to become self-sufficient in production and consumption; and suppression of individual property on the grounds that man becomes estranged from himself through the objects he acquires. Beginning with the production of *The Brig,* the Living Theatre strove to achieve a condition of genuine community work within the troupe. In 1968, five years after *The Brig's* premiere, Judith and Julian confessed that their community had not yet attained the ultimate state of development. The Living Theatre had been affirming more and more strongly its conviction that each one of us is personally responsible for the way things are in the world. One can easily understand the rage that seizes the Left when it is confronted with the declaration of something as "reactionary" as collective guilt. It is obvious that in having refused to point its finger at the guilty—especially in its European productions —and in having confined itself to occasional indications, in performance, of the degrees of man's guilt, the Living Theatre did not choose any easy alternative.

Non-violence need not be equated with futility; when its ways and means are sufficiently extended, seemingly impossible results can be achieved. "What would be more efficacious to end the war in Viet Nam than to organize a general strike across the territory of the United States and beyond it? The lack of money and the stopping of production is not tolerated for long by a state"—declare Judith and Julian. *The Brig* was an enactment of the opposite of non-violence: It aimed at destroying violence by representing it. The theatre became a place of evil, the actor no longer actor but victim or tormentor— a "sacrificial" presence, as invoked by Artaud. Judith Malina and Julian Beck often use the expression.

In preparing the production Judith also drew on

Piscator's emphasis on clarity and communicating and on Meyerhold: the brig is not only social structure, but a setting that directs action and wherein every detail, every object has meaning and function and serves a specific purpose within the action. It is a dehumanized place, demanding dehumanized conduct. It is a prison, *the* prison from which one never emerges once he has spent a few days behind its walls; at least, not until all prisons in the world have been torn down. Judith and Julian know this to be true.

Judith also drew on the material contained in the *Guidebook for Marines* that is issued to recruits. The Marine is given to understand that he is to obey, and not to reflect on the meaning of his actions. "You must kill, not simply defeat your opponent," Judith quotes.

The prisoners are called "maggots" by the guards; they are even refused the immediate gratification of purely biological needs. And who are these torturers? They are picked at random from the Marine Corps and trained. Nazi killers were amateurs, too. . . . Rehearsals as well as performances allowed for a certain margin of spontaneity to both guards and prisoners. A prisoner unwittingly stepping on a white line, for example, would evoke an immediate improvised act of punishment from a guard. Consequently, the actors were treading a tightrope that was, in effect, real. The blows may as well have been real, for their psychological effect on actors so involved invariably led to a real reaction, the contraction of muscles, and could not have been much more violent or painful. Inflections and subtle gestures were minutely analyzed, and authentic details were provided by Brown and actors who had been Marines themselves. The brig, and soon *The Brig,* turned into a monstrous creation; the actors had never felt more defenseless in their lives. The roles were being rotated, so that the actor playing, say, prisoner No. 5 one night would play a guard the night after. Their physical well-being was being threatened during any given performance. The troupe felt a relentless honesty, for the first time, and their reality was profoundly transmitted to the audience. The spectator remembered his own vulnerability, and the victim on the stage became his brother. Everything took place as in a ritual; it was not the purpose to "provoke," and commitment was total on both sides of the barbed wire.

Was it a representation of the real world? If it was, a group of Marines attending a performance thought otherwise: "Things were like that around 1956," they said, "but they have changed."

15 | AN INFORMAL ASSESSMENT

Has there been a clear line of evolution in the manner in which your productions in the United States were conceived through the years? I am, of course, excluding The Brig.

JULIAN: Judith and I discussed everything—direction, costumes, etc. During the first years we prepared everything in advance. Then, little by little, we began to let scenery and direction *emerge* from the play. When rehearsals started, I would hold my tongue if she was directing, and she would do the same if I was. As time went on, Judith allowed greater and greater freedom for the actor, thereby introducing greater creativity. She rendered the action comprehensible and coherent for the actor; after that, the actor was able to move and to contrive things on his own. From a certain point on during rehearsals he would know more about the character, about the role, than the director.

In 1962 or 1963, I was asked to give a quick definition of the work of the Living Theatre. Almost without thinking, I said that our aim was to increase conscious awareness, to stress the sacredness of life, to break down the walls. All our plays have underlined these three objectives. From the technical and directional point of view, our work was traditional in comparison to what we began to do later, with *Frankenstein*—collective direction. *The Brig* opened many doors for us, indeed. When we established ourselves in Europe, on the impetus of *The Brig*, we began to talk freely about politics and about the world, and the troupe took up political, social, and even economic positions that were quite different. At the same time, the acting itself began to change because, you see, before that we did not know *what* to change in it.

16 | THOSE OCTOBER DAYS—1963

The Living Theatre was to experience the persecution depicted in *The Brig* even more acutely in real life. "When the revolution comes no one gets hurt but all the money gets burned," Julian once wrote. Meanwhile, however, money was taking devastating revenge on them.

The Brig had been running for five months—thanks, in part, to the one-time-only services of a press agent Julian hired during June and July of 1963 to counteract unfavorable reviews in the dailies—when an eviction order arrived. The company owed $4,500 in back rent. The understanding landlord had obtained the order several months earlier but delayed serving it. In September, Julian had pledged him the furnishings and air-conditioning—worth between six and ten thousand dollars—hoping that it represented a tacit understanding of patience on the landlord's part. Three weeks later, on October 16th, the eviction order was served. The landlord's attorney gave them an extension until the 22nd, during which perhaps they might raise the money. Julian called a press conference for the 18th, and no sooner was it over than the Internal Revenue Service descended on them and proceeded to seize the theatre, declaring it to be government property in lieu of $28,435.10 owed in taxes, insurances and penalties. The Becks had never contested the taxes charged to them while they had been engaged in trying to obtain tax exemption all along. Julian estimated that they had paid something like $75,000 in taxes over the years. Since 1959, the first year they were unable to pay the tax on time, their dialogue with the IRS had become quite lively. (At the trial the IRS said that 77 letters were exchanged between the Living Theatre and them during those years!) They were simply unable to put aside enough for taxes from box office receipts. "If we had operated this way we would certainly have had to close *The Connection* and *The Brig* the very weeks they opened. In fact, we would have had to close the whole theatre years ago. It was a matter of insisting on art before money, before risk, before any other obligation. Any other obligation except one of life, death, physical harm. . . ."[1]

The Becks pleaded with the IRS agents to be allowed to perform during the coming weekend. A closed theatre cannot take in money, and the actors were penniless. The agents remained inflexible.

The actors got wind of the proceedings. Steve Thompson decided not to leave the premises. A sit-in began. The actors wanted a chance at least to find other jobs before closing the theatre. "IRS asked us to ask them to leave. How could we? We had been telling them to do just this for years. There were more than a dozen and if we had asked them to leave I am not sure they would have. Proud of it."[2]

The IRS sealed all doors, except the offices. While faithful friends were picketing outside, displaying placards demanding the preservation of the Living Theatre, Judith went inside for an urgently needed tampon only to find her dressing room padlocked. She asked about a dozen agents to open it, but all refused. Julian knew that Judith was not indulging a whim, and also made the request. Again, it was denied. Julian thereupon lifted the door off its hinges, went in, and got the tampon. The first incident. The IRS men took pictures of the violated door.

[1] Julian Beck in *Tulane Review, op. cit.*
[2] *Ibid.*

The actors stayed inside, because they would not be able to return if they left. Only newspapermen could cross the barriers with impunity. That night the IRS men decided to leave, and told the Becks they could stay, provided they did not touch the seals or use any objects impounded by the government. The Becks went home, after deciding to give a performance of *The Brig* in the lobby and calling a rehearsal for two o'clock Saturday. They left two or three friends behind to picket the theatre.

The sit-in continued on Friday, and the lobby was rearranged. In the afternoon Julian sat on the stairs, physically blocking them, to prevent the IRS men from taking his personal papers. Actors who had to go to the bathroom had to put up with a two-man escort. Julian then discovered an entrance to the projection room: a movable panel for fire emergency exit. He also found another emergency exit. Both led into the theatre and both were not sealed. The company decided to give the last performance in the theatre itself, since it did not involve breaking any seals.

On Saturday at 7:45 p.m., the actors gathered behind the set they had restored after it had been dismantled by the IRS men. The IRS men did not allow the audience to enter, but some reporters and spectators, a good many, got in by climbing a ladder. The police arrived. Meanwhile, others crossed a roof and entered through a window. At 9:45, the play began. The IRS men declined the invitation to watch, but they did not interrupt the show.

The performance was, in Julian's words, "in and of itself an act of civil disobedience. It was not a message play, not a play about protest, it was a real protest against a life in which everything is measured by Mammon's thumb," an "anarchist direct action."

Kenneth Brown took part in it, and there were forty spectators and reporters along with about thirty actors. Afterward, the IRS men asked everyone to leave. The Becks pleaded with them to allow two benefit performances on Sunday for the actors, but they were adamant: "We are only following orders." Judith responded with the remark that after Eichmann this was not an excuse. Thereupon the IRS men delivered their ultimatum. Twenty-five actors, spectators, friends were arrested, two by mistake, at one-thirty Sunday morning. The six women were taken to the Women's House of Detention, the nineteen men to the Federal Prison on West Street. ("A real Hilton," Julian remarked later. He vowed to commit only federal crimes so that he would be incarcerated there.)

On Sunday, the IRS men emptied the theatre of its contents, including the barbed wire, asking themselves if the proceeds from the sale would pay for the cost of removal. The sale brought two hundred and sixty-seven dollars.

That evening the twenty-five were released, the Becks and two friends on five-hundred-dollar bail each. A few months later, everything was to fall apart.

17 | INFLEXIBLE LAW

Irving Maidman, an entrepreneur with vast real estate holdings in Manhattan, invited the Becks to use his Midway theatre rent free (but changed his mind and insisted on rent later on, a betrayal which ended the engagement, for it was impossible to pay both rent and actors' salaries).

And in January, 1964, while still performing *The Brig* under the banner of "Exile Productions" at Maidman's West 42nd Street Theatre, the Becks were indicted by a federal grand jury for "impeding a federal officer in the pursuit of his duties." The Becks were accused of having refused to leave the theatre and of having attempted to recover a seized object (a sewing machine belonging to Julian's mother). In addition, Julian was accused of having forced open a sealed door, of having blocked a stairway, of having offered a ladder for the audience to get in, and of having used a seized mimeograph machine belonging to the lighting man for preparing a press release—all of them acts that Julian himself characterized as minor misdemeanors in the course of the proceedings. He declared toward the end of the trial, "Your Honor, I have watched the majesty of the United States degraded and demeaned by trivia that are beyond belief. I have seen the law of this country lose all of its dignity."

The trial got under way in mid-May and lasted ten days. Retaining a lawyer would have implied the acceptance of the system and the tacit acknowledgment of the view that innocence cannot defend itself. Julian had seen Orson Welles's *The Lady from*

Shanghai and conducted the case as Bannister would have, without the banter. The Becks had no desire to defend themselves; they wanted to talk to Judge Palmieri and the jury as to human beings, despite the advice of their court-assigned attorney. They were trying to establish a dialogue with the jurors in the hope of clearly displaying their points of view and, thereby, conveying their own values. They never admitted having done any wrong.[1]

Tennessee Williams, Edward Albee, their son Garry, Julian's mother, all testified to their moral integrity. The Becks did not utilize the proceedings to build themselves into martyrs; what they did was simply to keep the whole matter on extralegal grounds, to stress the importance of their work and explain their concept of theater. Judith had occasion to talk about law at some length:

> The Germany in which my father was brought up was a free country but it changed its nature, it changed its laws, and the laws became more and more rigid and the laws no longer left room

[1] Good faith was to be Julian's only weapon on another occasion. The publisher of *The Brig* found the script too short for a book and asked the Becks for two separate essays to accompany it. In reading the proofs of his essay, "Storming the Barricades," Julian discovered more than six hundred alterations. It became, in his words, "Mr. Beck in clean clothes, Mr. Beck as gentleman, Mr. Beck without reefer." He asked for the restoration of his text,, but in vain. He barely managed to have a preface added, dated in prison (January, 1965), where he said, among other things: "I am an anarchist. I don't sue, I don't get injunctions, I advocate revolution. (. . .) Literary fights always look funny five years later. So will this." (The publisher's alterations, aside from a few deletions, were chiefly matters of punctuation and the like, but they made all the difference in the world to Julian, between Julian Beck speaking directly to someone and Julian Beck "writing an essay.")

(. . .) I am not suggesting that we have come to such a terrible pass. Pray to God that we never shall. But the rigidity of the law and the unwillingness of the law to change and yield to human feeling, this seems to me the crucial point at which tyranny begins.

When those who say, "at this point the law is wrong," can no longer say it (. . .), when we come to that point when a person can no longer say, "I am an anarchist, I believe in a law of love, and I believe that the laws of love could be sufficient to organize human life in a beautiful and meaningful way without punishment and harm," as long as I can say that, I am living in a free land. (. . .)

We told you about how we had built that theatre, how the stage that I was carried off from that night I had nailed together with my own hands. (. . .) We did the work and we loved the work and here it was gone, and here it was over.

We were in mourning for our theatre, and we were in shock, and we decided to say, "No, don't take it away from us. We love it." We were saying no to the rigid letter of the law and yet trying at every point to do no harm, and we still don't see how putting on that performance that Saturday night really hurt anybody except the pride of the rigidity of the law (. . .). And I appeal to you to understand that we do not believe that we committed a crime. (. . .) You have heard us say that we believed that what we did was right and good. But the law's nature is to be rigid and to define, and then it is up to the human heart, which is not rigid unless it is dead.

Judith and Julian spoke in everyday language throughout, ignoring legal terminology consistently, even though they had spent considerable time poring over law books. Judge Palmieri had generous praise for the thoroughness of their preparation of the case.

On May 25th, after several hours of deliberation, the jury of eleven men and one woman found the Becks guilty. This was too much. As soon as the word "guilty" was spoken in the reading of the verdict, Judith declared in a calm, strong voice, "Innocent!" She was ordered to keep quiet. "You can't stop me from claiming my innocence!" she persisted. "You can cut out my tongue, but you can't stop me from declaring that I am innocent. I do not give you that privilege, Sir!" (To the great consternation of Judith and Julian, the newspaper headlines said: "Judith Malina Wants to Be Killed.")

When Judith cried out "Innocent!" Julian, together with several members of the troupe and other friends who were among the spectators, followed suit, whereupon the judge told the Becks that they were liable to contempt of court charges. Nevertheless, he assured them that they would not be sent to jail.

The charges contained in the indictment would have entailed a total maximum sentence of thirty-one years in prison and fines of $46,000, had they been found guilty on all counts. As it happened, the jury found against Julian on seven counts and against Judith on three. He now faced a maximum of nineteen years in prison and a $26,000 fine, and she eight years and a $10,500 fine. In addition, the Living Theatre Corporation was also found guilty on five counts.

Judith and Julian wished to be sentenced immediately, but the judge told them not to worry and set sentencing for June 5th. Having pledged to appear in court that day, they were released. When

June 5th duly arrived, Judith was sentenced to thirty days, Julian to sixty, and the Living Theatre Corporation fined $2,500. Acknowledging the information that the company had a contractual obligation to perform in London, the judge prevailed upon the prosecutor to permit it to fulfill the contract. Bail was set at $1,000 for Julian and $500 for Judith, and both were released.

During the course of the trial, the Becks conducted themselves exactly as they have anywhere else, under any other set of circumstances. They revealed the same naïveté, the same faith in human nature, the same wonderful vitality. In all sincerity, they advised the IRS agents to take off their ties, and pleaded with them to try to live a more meaningful life. The jury did not take these gestures into account, of course.

Good faith was to be Julian's only weapon on another occasion. The publisher of *The Brig* found the script too short for a book and asked the Becks for two separate essays to accompany it. In reading the proofs of his essay, "Storming the Barricades," Julian discovered more than six hundred alterations. It became, in his words, "Mr. Beck in clean clothes, Mr. Beck as gentleman, Mr. Beck without reefer." He asked for the restoration of his text, but in vain. He barely managed to have a preface added, dated in prison (January, 1965), where he said, among other things: "I am an anarchist. I don't sue, I don't get injunctions, I advocate revolution. (. . .) Literary fights always look funny five years later. So will this." (The publisher's alterations, aside from a few deletions, were chiefly matters of punctuation and the like, but they made all the difference in the world to Julian, between Julian Beck speaking directly to someone and Julian Beck "writing an essay.")

The company went to London in the summer of 1964 and presented *The Brig* for several weeks.[2]

[2] After London, sensing that for some time the

Then the group created *Mysteries and Smaller Pieces* in Paris and performed it during November in Brussels, Antwerp, Basel, and Berlin; at the end of November they sought refuge in a farmhouse in Heist-sur-Mer, Belgium, and remained there until early February, 1965. However, Judith and Julian had to return to New York in mid-December to serve their sentences. Judith left the Passaic County Jail on January 13th and rejoined the company in Heist after a crossing aboard the *Queen Elizabeth*. Julian was freed from Danbury Federal Penitentiary on February 12th and arrived in Brussels the following day. Both had spent their time in prison working on future projects; Judith prepared for the staging of *The Maids* and Julian designed the sets. Meanwhile, *The New York Times* published letters from Julian in which he discussed the theatre, as always, or life, or the world as it was and as it ought to be; he spoke of the prison as a pleasant place where one had everything one needed to cultivate the mind, where the food was good and one could even enjoy the outdoors. In all, it was not unlike life, with the difference that one knew one was in prison.

The nightmare was over. A year later, *The Trial of Judith Malina and Julian Beck*, directed by Tom Bissinger with music by Jackson MacLow, was scheduled at the La Mama Experimental Theatre. An expression of respect by friends. . . .

European public would demonstrate an exceptional interest in their work, as it already had done in 1961 and 1962, the Living Theatre decided to spend more time in Europe. The European press spoke of a troupe chased from the United States for extremist political positions. How could a government chase its own citizens from its shores? It would have to mean that the citizens were deprived of their nationality, which was not the case. The Living Theatre chose its exile.

18

MYSTERIES AND SMALLER PIECES

The exile in Europe had begun.

In October, 1964, the Living Theatre was looking for a place in Paris in which to hold rehearsals, for the Becks were thinking about staging *The Balcony* and *The Maids*. The American Center for Students and Artists on the Boulevard Raspail extended its hospitality to the company, in return for which the actors agreed to present an evening of entertainment. They did not want to do an excerpt from the plays in rehearsal, nor did they want to do *The Brig*. Thus, on October 26th the audience of students and artists witnessed the creation of *Mysteries and Smaller Pieces* on the stage. It was never to be performed in exactly that way again; there was to be a temporary second version, and finally a third, definitive one.

It is the third version that will be described here, as completely as possible. The nine distinct scenes that constitute the play do not follow one another in random sequence but form a coherent entity, each breeding the subsequent one, each unfolding in the same order at every performance.

Judith and Julian chose the nine scenes from among some twenty they had at their disposal.

Each scene lasts five to fifteen minutes, except the last scene in Part Two. (It may be noted at this point that *Mysteries* has caused more of a stir than any other of the Living Theatre's European productions.)

Part One

1. *"The Brig Dollar."* Death, vertical rigidity, life "frozen," man deprived of movement, the military. An actor stands at attention on an empty stage, completely motionless, lit from the side only, his vertical immobility a projected reply to the horizontal rigidity of corpses heaped up on stage like a pile of wood at the end of the performance. After a few minutes—the receptiveness of the audience determines how many—several actors, escaped from *The Brig,* march on stage in step from the back of the auditorium. The first one transforms himself into a corporal and distributes cleaning utensils among the others. Everything is mimed; the men scrub, wash, put up clotheslines on the stage as well as in the auditorium, and do exercises in formation. They are mechanical puppets working on completely useless tasks, moving about aimlessly, no more alive than the imperturbable actor who continues to stand at attention throughout the scene. Their arrival symbolizes the intrusion of the contemporary world, with all its aberrations. . . .

In the auditorium, actors who are not participating in the scene recite a poem of John Harriman's—a young American poet who became devoted to the work of the Living Theatre and has been with the troupe for some time. The poem is an assemblage of all words and numbers to be found on a dollar bill, including the signatures. The general idea for this scene—money as the engine of the world's folly—came from Henry Howard, one of the members of the company. The scene ends, as does *The Brig,* with a sonorous "Yes, Sir!" Only in this piece the response is transposed into humor by the fact that it becomes a retort to an utterly incomprehensible order spluttered by the corporal.

2. *"The Raga."* The theatre is plunged into darkness and silence, as if it had never witnessed the

extraordinary activities of the first scene. A voice rises up—a woman's voice, accompanied by a guitar—and chants a Hindu raga for several minutes. One of the troupe's actresses who frequently sings *ragas* provided the basis for the scene. The *raga* is improvised at each performance. It may be appropriate to note here that the Living Theatre used improvisation as a technique of acting in *Mysteries* but it also utilized improvisation as a technique of discovery during rehearsal for *Antigone* and *Paradise Now*. The chant, the woman, the pleasure to the ears and eyes, the Living Theatre turns its back on a dehumanized civilization and reconquers the lost delights of the senses. A chant of the body, a chant of the individual, a chant of the community, eventually, then the inability to cope with and sustain sensual pleasure, and the return to rigidity. For that is what the scene is about: the world as it is.

3. *"Odiferie."* Having delighted the ears, the troupe turns to the pleasures of smelling. Incandescent tips of incense sticks, held at arm's length by each actor, glow in the dark. The lights go on in the auditorium and the actors, lined up abreast, advance very slowly toward the spectators and enfold them in clouds of incense. (Nicola Cernovich had been directing the lighting for the Living Theatre during the past few years, as well as for Paul Taylor's and Merce Cunningham's troupes. Once he performed a happening called "Odiferie" during which he wandered through the auditorium carrying incense sticks. Julian thought then of using the idea in a Living Theatre event.)

4. *"Street Songs."* The ceremony of incense is followed by a political interrogation. The actors douse their incense sticks and pile them in a heap. Julian remains seated in center stage, all alone, illuminated by a vertical spotlight. He announces, " 'Street Songs,' by Jackson MacLow." It seems now that the ceremony has been raised to a level of incantation, of prayer. The meaning of the prayer—

a true prayer which asks for something—is implicit: "How can we change the world?"

But "Street Songs" is concerned with the *what,* not the *how.* What Julian is saying is, "Find a way. . . . Make it work. . . ." The *how* is left unanswered. What is to be attained is the end to war—of which Vietnam is but a current manifestation; the end of money, to banks, to police, to the army, to military service, to the state, to prisons. Bread for the poor, freedom for all.

MacLow's poem—to which Julian added supplications of his own—is constructed in the manner of Christian litanies and Hindu *mantras.* The litany is recited, usually, only in the language of the audience to which the troupe is playing. Actors are seated among the spectators, and they repeat Julian's words at regular intervals, now loudly, now softly. The Living Theatre would like to have, more than anything else, participation of the public, which sometimes occurs. Several techniques have been tried (e.g., different tones of voice) but so far none has given full satisfaction.

(Jackson MacLow, whose name occurs so often in this chronicle, was born in Chicago in 1922. He is a musician and poet, as well as a licensed teacher of Greek. He has been participating in civil rights and peace movements since 1939, and became an anarchist in 1945. For the past fifteen years he has been keenly interested in the mechanism of chance, which interest is expressed in his poetry, his plays, his music. He has been a member of the Living Theatre for several years as actor, composer, and author of *The Marrying Maiden.*)

5. *"The Chord."* This scene supplies the answer to the question posed in "Street Songs," with a simple harmony and collective beauty that could bind together members of an anarchist society. The meaning of the scene is reinforced by the actual fact that the Living Theatre is in the process of becom-

ing an anarchist community itself. In the chant the actors form a circle, including Julian therein. They hold each other by the shoulders. The vertical spotlight used in the preceding scene denotes the boundaries of the circle. They inhale deeply. One of the actors in the circle intones a sound; then the nearest ones listen attentively to that sound and intone sounds of their own; each actor listens with total intensity, while beginning his own sound, to the sounds on his immediate right and left. The chord swells in intensity and volume, then descends gently and fades away. The quality of listening will determine the quality of the response, and the harmony and beauty of the ensemble. The chord is entirely improvised at each performance.

(The idea for this scene is credited to Joseph Chaikin, who acted with the Living Theatre, most notably as Galy Gay in *Man Is Man,* before striking out on his own. He founded the Open Theatre in New York in 1963, and achieved notable successes with *America Hurrah!* and *Viet Rock.* With Chaikin, the chord has been used mainly in exercises; for the Living Theatre it became a "coming together" device; a profound expression of belonging to the community: the human community in general, the company in particular. When an actor returns after an absence, his reintegration is symbolized in the ceremony of the chord.)

6. *"The Djdjdj."* The last scene in Part One is another reply to the question "How to change the world?" How? By eliminating everything that is polluted. This solution is represented once again in the form of an image both mental and physical. The form is a yoga breathing exercise. Six actors sit at the front of the stage. They blow their noses at length in pieces of paper torn from a roll; having rid themselves of impurities, they breathe deeply through the nose, inhaling and exhaling, attaining mastery of body and spirit. They kneel and bring their heads very rapidly from back to front, then remain immo-

bile, their eyes bulging, their tongues hanging out. A drawn out sound of "djdjdjdjdjdj . . ." emitted by a convulsing actor terminates their concentration.

(Steve Ben Israel originated this scene; he was one of the first among the troupe to take up yoga. It is interesting that when a roll of toilet paper—an object of shame, in Europe at least—was used in this scene—the public was scandalized. If a wider roll of paper—a wasteful substitute—had been used, no one would have paid any attention to it. A very curious reaction.)

Part Two

7. *"Tableaux Vivants."* The troupe continues to pay homage to the body and celebrates here the sense of sight in this scene. A wood structure occupies the center of the stage; it is divided into four vertical compartments facing the audience. The structure is perhaps twelve inches deep, seven feet high, and twelve feet wide. Illuminated only by footlights for periods of a few seconds at a time, the actors group into tableaux vivants in front of the structure and in its compartments. They work in teams of four, with the other actors concealed behind the structure. The makeup of the teams changes all the time, and each team is captured by the lights in ten to twenty tableaux. Always improvising, the actors assume completely unexpected postures, grouping in twos or threes or remaining solitary. None of the postures is ever foreseen. If an actor is used as a prop by another while he forms his next posture in the dark, nobody has any idea about the position assumed by the actor thus used, or the effect it produces.

The miniature masterpieces flash by in total silence. The faces of the actors express rage, horror, joy, indifference, boredom, concentration. "All we want to say with these tableaux vivants," Julian comments, "is that whatever posture our bodies assume, it will always be beautiful, because the body is beautiful and the eye finds a natural satisfaction in looking at it."

(Julian conceived the idea for this scene when he saw a comedian in a packing case someone left behind on the stage of the American Center in Paris. He was greatly surprised when he discovered, in the Italian magazine *Sipario*, Eli Lotard's photograph of an earlier Artaud staging of similar tableaux vivants.)

8. *"Sound and Movement."* About ten actors form two lines, one on each side of the stage, from front to back, facing each other. One of them improvises a movement and a sound, and directs them both toward another actor who observes them, takes them, and quickly or slowly transforms them into another sound and movement before passing them on. When an actor hits upon a sound and gesture that wins the consent of all they are adopted by all, and the scene ends in a state of collective delight, a deeper sort of communication, once again.

(Joseph Chaikin devised this exercise, and his pupil Lee Worley taught it to the Living Theatre.)

9. *"The Plague."* The preceding scene represents the closest form of harmony and cooperation; this one is its exact opposite. It goes on for about half an hour. Using a phrase of Artaud's, Julian calls it the "double" of "Sound and Movement," or, in Cocteau's term, "the other side of the mirror." It is the negative counterpart of Scene 8. No more interaction, no more community. Death reigns everywhere.

The scene was inspired by Artaud's description of the great plague that devastated Marseille in 1720. The actors, shrouded in dim light, groan and cry out in the grip of the dreadful disease, wrestling death. Long-repressed vices are suddenly awakened in the tormented wretches and they try to possess their fellow-victims, rolling like erupting lava all over the stage and the auditorium. But soon, death prevails over them. Then, very slowly, a few survivors rise up; in silence, they remove the boots of the dead, line them up in the front of the stage, and heap the corpses into the well-defined shape of a wood pile. The light, which has been becoming more intense, now goes out in the auditorium and then very slowly comes up on the stage where the gravediggers await their turn; they are erect, but having arisen from among the dead, are "the dead burying the dead." The last image that registers on the eye is the pile of corpses, a small dented pyramid from which all life seems to have withdrawn forever. Whether it symbolizes specific death—the concentration camp or war itself—is of small import.

The dying have fought death in isolation. They will not meet ever again, except in death where no interaction exists. They have died of the plague, the symbol of everything that prevents the world from breathing. The troupe reproduces a horizontal image of the rigid soldier in "The Brig Dollar"—an image that, after what has just transpired, is more startling in itself and more natural than the vertical, for the dead are buried lying down.

(The idea for this scene was conceived by Julian.)

Mysteries and Smaller Pieces—the title was coined by Judith[1]—was performed on a totally empty stage, in everyday clothes of the actors' choice. In *Mysteries* the actors don't experience stage fright because they know that if the audience has the Power they, the actors, will end with the Plague and at that time, whatever may have happened during the performance, silence will prevail and the spectator will be seized. It is the Plague that "carries" and supports the actor during the play, that gives him this impassibility, this superior resistance.

The play has been presented in other versions, which we will now comment upon.

[1] Judith is here making allusion to Eleusis and the rites which were celebrated, of greater or lesser importance according to their category.

19

EIGHT-YEAR-OLD KIDS

The first performance of Mysteries *in Paris did not end with the plague scene. You concluded it with what you have called "Free theatre."*

JUDITH: We were preparing for *Frankenstein* at the time and we chose a theme that was related to it: horror in all its manifestations. The actors were free to improvise completely after the "Sound and Movement" scene, and we had an organ. It served us well. Also, we produced every possible sound with the furnishings of the theatre itself—the floor, the seats, partitions, what have you. We were "playing" the room. There were forty of us and this first "free theatre" in our history went on for something like three hours. A great many spectators took part in it, and it spilled out into the auditorium, the lobby, the street. It was a rather "sophisticated" audience, lots of young actors, musicians, and students; the type of people who would participate in that kind of activity. Some of them performed "choices" that were really beautiful and absorbing, although some were sort of extravagant, more foolish than horrible. But when you do "free theatre," you cannot say that this is bad and this is good. Besides, there you have the biggest difficulty, the absence of criteria.

What memories did the company preserve of that evening?

JUDITH: There were endless discussions about it for a whole year. Anger, nervousness, desire to do it again, determination never to do it again because it was disgusting and so on. Finally, by overall consensus, we decided not to talk about it any more, so as to appease everyone. Looking back on it now, it seems to us that it had some rather astounding moments. For example, the audience piled the seats into a high mountain, and one of them, an actor, I think, climbed up on the stage and shouted very loudly and repeatedly, "Fuck your mother," like a fascist screaming in a murderous rage. The lighting was manipulated by a number of people and broke down. One of the actors followed the people who were leaving and told them in an anguished voice, "Please, don't die!"

JULIAN: Trouble is that when a spectator in a "free theatre" shouts "Fuck your mother," it is an idea rather than a burst of creative sound.

JUDITH: But it was a spectator, Julian!

JULIAN: True, but I think that this is perhaps the right time to discuss the "actor." In the contemporary theatre we assume that the actor has prepared his work over a long period of time. He must have summoned up during the process of his preparations something that belongs to him alone in the context of his role, something he can repeat at will by going back to the original inspiration. But this is based on the level of conscious interpretation; the actor has not made himself truly free to make the "trip," he is not truly inspired. This is also what often happens during the "happenings"; people draw almost entirely on their conscious experiences. At the Living Theatre, we think it is necessary to attain a state of inspiration, what we sometimes call a "trance."[1] The improvised rehearsals of *Antigone* started out that way. According to this concept, spectators were not witnesses at the process of rehearsal but shared in the creative adventure, helped in the creation itself. It's a question of depth. If the

[1] Drugs: "I believe that the bourgeois governments have forbidden them because they are afraid and want everybody to remain in the prison in which we live permanently. Perhaps what one learns with drugs is more real than what one learns with the drug of education, of politics, of language, of words." (Julian Beck.)

actor is not merely piecing his role together, if he is not content with displaying his competence, his artistic taste, his knowledge—effective things which he knows are funny, shocking, or what have you—in brief, if he really achieves a state of liberation so that the theatrical "trip" may be undertaken, then we can speak of true inspiration. Then we have some chance to inspire poetry in the audience—and I am talking about the people who act like eight-year-old kids when they go to see *Mysteries*.

JUDITH: I don't think, in spite of all that, that it is possible to obtain a satisfactory response from a whole audience under actual conditions. At least not unless one plays to a church-going type of audience, to people who respond with dignity because they are inhibited and because that's what they're there for, or else for an audience at a very high artistic level, a level which is conceivable only in a world where the revolution has already taken place; a post-revolutionary world where there is no war, no exploitation of any kind. Paradise! As for the "non-paradisiac" audience, which is the only kind we can legitimately speak about, it will respond in an idiotic fashion for the most part, because that is the truth of these people's lives, because these are the people who work, who run after money, who live in a world of war, who have no real hope. . . . It is possible to touch a whole audience at certain moments, or a segment of an audience all the time, or a segment at certain moments, but it is not possible to elevate the response of a whole audience at all times. True, there are circumstances when everyone becomes inspired, but these are rare. I believe that there are also certain people who can be led to where you want them, because they feel warmly toward you, and if you are there, they are there with you. Obviously, I am talking about an ideal relationship. The fact that a receptive public exists proves that one must continue in this way, that there is a cause that makes it worth while to pursue our goal.

JULIAN: It makes it imperative.

As a postscript to this interview, a follow-up of events shows that the Living Theatre did not permit any "free theatre" sessions again. The plague scene was present when *Mysteries* was revived; at first it was framed by a poem written by Judith under the influence of Artaud's *Le Theatre et son double,* with each actor reciting one line a predetermined number of times, but not at any predetermined point in the action, and then lying down on the stage. An organ was heard offstage, playing slowly and mournfully; four actors rose up, piled up the corpses, then vanished. At the Amsterdam performance in February, 1965, and for several months afterward, *Mysteries* ended following the plague scene with a "free jazz" session performed by three actors, Piet Kuiters, Steve Ben Israel, and Barry Schuck. Then Piet Kuiters left the company and no more "free jazz" sessions followed.

In an interview in the *Paris Gazette* on October 18, 1964, Judith made the following statement: "The theatre we come from considered the audience a collective. Now we are getting to a theatre where the audience is treated as individualized, as in a sex relationship. A sex relationship must free us from convention. This nakedness and trust in bed is what the actor must come to when we break through and personalize the audience." She was in agreement with Julian who wrote once: "I don't like to work alone, I adore collaboration, to join with someone and to do something, much more gratifying than working alone, because something else is happening, it's very sexy, even when you are not really fucking, you are filling someone else, and someone else is filling or is filled by you."

20

ANALOGIES

Mysteries ignored traditions more blithely than any previous production of the Living Theatre by having no sets, no costumes, no text. In this play, which was a real manifesto, all precautionary rhetoric was absent, and the program given out to the audience was thoroughly laconic. The newspapers referred to the production as "provocation, pure and simple," "bad joke," and "farce." Part of the public, misled by press comments, saw an opportunity for instant gratification and went to the theatre in order to make animal-like noises, to whistle and call out remarks in bad taste. The "bourgeoisie" felt personally insulted and if they could have banned the production, they would have done it.

What was it that made *Mysteries* such a unique experience? It clothed itself in a language that resembled the phrasing of religious rites—Christian and Hindu. But this language was being used on a stage, and part of the public—those who regard being "taken in" as the supreme insult, feeling reviled by "lack of respect"—felt that certain revered traditions were being profaned in their presence. Hence the violent reactions, the virtual contest of abuse indulged in by certain elements in the audience.

The words "sect," "ceremony," "mystical," "symbol," "communion," "rite" recurred all too frequently in published and private criticisms of the piece. Why? The objective pursued by the Living Theatre lies in the use of secular means—the theatre—and ordinary wisdom to achieve a livable world. Establishment theatre on the other hand, with

1. *Mysteries.*
The Chord scene.

2

3

2. *Mysteries.*
The Brig Dollar scene.

3. *Mysteries.*
The Plague scene.

4

5

6

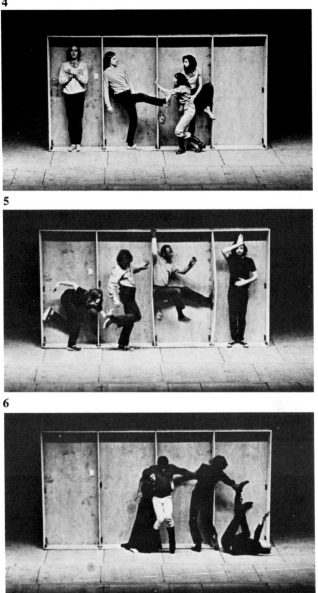

4–6. *Mysteries.*
Three Tableaux Vivants.

7. Rufus Collins.

8. Mary Mary.

9. Frank Hoogeboom.

10. Petra Vogt and Birgit Knabe.

11. Judith Malina.

12. Judith Malina and Isha Manna.

13. Julian Beck.

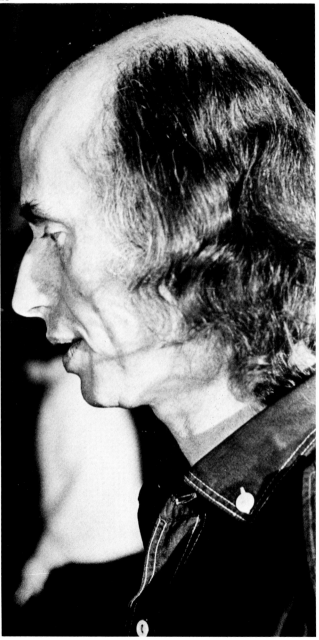

14. Sketch by Judith Malina for *Frankenstein.*

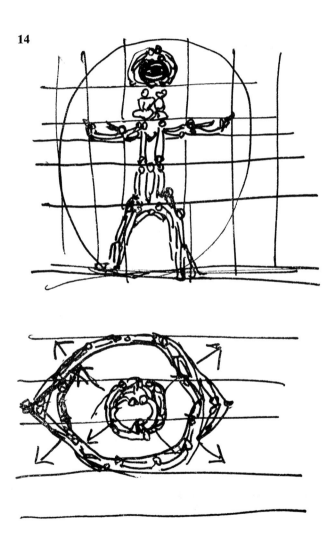

15–16. *Frankenstein.*
The victim tries to escape but is trapped.

15

16

17

17. *Frankenstein.*
Actors face the audience.

18. Frankenstein about to
remove the victim's heart.

19

20

19. *Frankenstein.*
Petra Vogt at control booth.

20. *Frankenstein.*
Inscriptions of various
parts of the head.

21. Frankenstein paints mystic signs on corpse.

21

22. *Frankenstein.*
The Creature.

23. *Frankenstein.*
The Legend of Buddha.

24. *Frankenstein.*
The cross of the Four Horsemen of the Apocalypse.

25. *Frankenstein.*
The Creature frees itself.

23

24

25

26. *Frankenstein.*
Jenny Hecht, victim of the electric chair, during a break.

27. *Frankenstein.*
The Ego has been expelled from the head.

28. *Frankenstein.*
Death rides an imaginary mount.

27

28

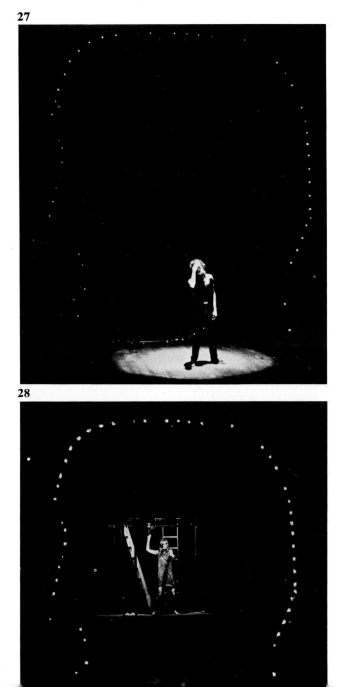

29. *Frankenstein.*
Madness reigns: World Action.

29

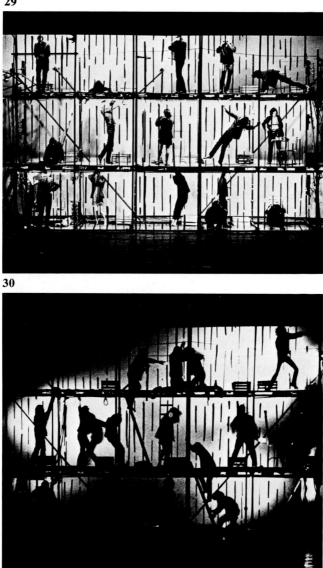

30

30. *Frankenstein.*
The fire begins.

31. *Frankenstein.*
Silhouette of Creáture re-forms behind structure.

32. *Antigone.*
Kreon with body of Polyneikes.

33. *Antigone.*
Kreon's body on ground, Polyneikes floats away triumphantly.

34

35

34. Antigone encountering four groups of Thebans.

35. Antigone carried off by guard.

36

37

36. *Antigone.*
Chant of the choir bemoaning man's actions.

37. *Antigone.*
Kreon emasculating Polyneikes.

38. *Antigone.*
Dispersal of the House of Oedipus and destruction of Thebes.

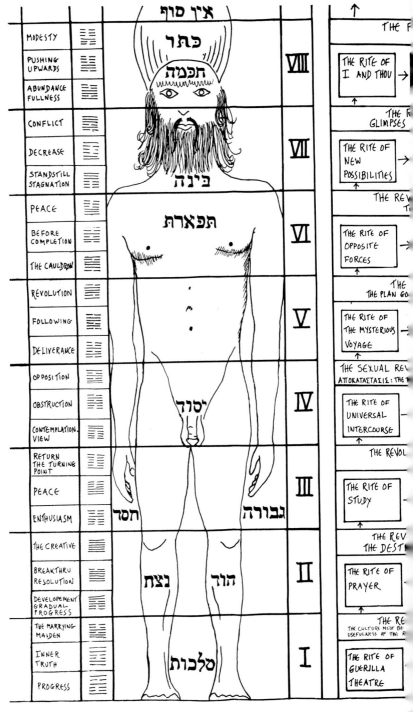

MODESTY	☷☶		
PUSHING UPWARDS	☷☴		
ABUNDANCE FULLNESS	☳☲	VIII	
CONFLICT	☰☵		
DECREASE	☶☱	VII	
STANDSTILL STAGNATION	☰☷		
PEACE	☷☰		
BEFORE COMPLETION	☲☵	VI	
THE CAULDRON	☲☴		
REVOLUTION	☱☲		
FOLLOWING	☱☳	V	
DELIVERANCE	☳☵		
OPPOSITION	☲☱		
OBSTRUCTION	☵☶	IV	
CONTEMPLATION. VIEW	☴☷		
RETURN THE TURNING POINT	☷☳		
PEACE	☷☰	III	
ENTHUSIASM	☳☷		
THE CREATIVE	☰☰		
BREAKTHRU RESOLUTION	☱☰	II	
DEVELOPEMENT GRADUAL PROGRESS	☴☶		
THE MARRYING MAIDEN	☳☱		
INNER TRUTH	☴☱	I	
PROGRESS	☲☷		

אין סוף

כתר

חכמה

בינה

תפארת

יסוד

חסד

גבורה

נצח

הוד

מלכות

THE F

THE RITE OF
I AND THOU →

THE F
GLIMPSES

THE RITE OF
NEW
POSSIBILITIES →

THE REV

THE RITE OF
OPPOSITE
FORCES →

THE
THE PLAN GO

THE RITE OF
THE MYSTERIOUS →
VOYAGE

THE SEXUAL REV
ΑΠΟΚΑΤΑΣΤΑΣΙΣ : THE

THE RITE OF
UNIVERSAL
INTERCOURSE →

THE REVOL

THE RITE OF
STUDY –

THE REV
THE DEST

THE RITE OF
PRAYER

THE RE
THE CULTURE MUST BE
USEFULNESS OF THE R

THE RITE OF
GUERILLA
THEATRE

39-40   THIS CHART IS THE MAP   THE ESSENTIAL TRIP I

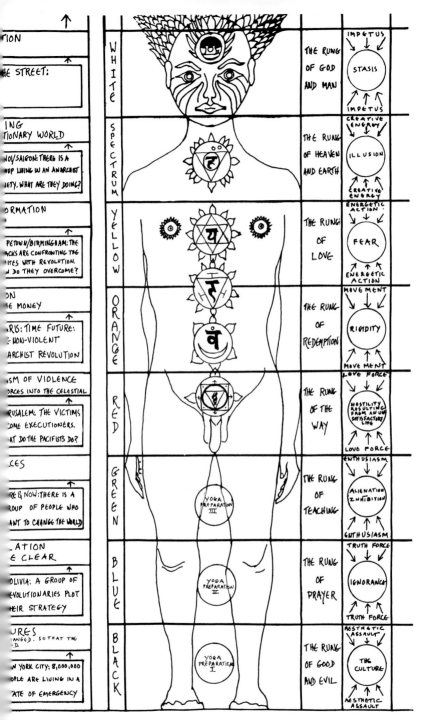

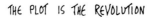

41. *Paradise Now*.
Rung 1, Vision 1.

42. *Paradise Now*.
Rung 1, Scene 1. "Don't step on the Indians."

43. *Paradise Now*.
Rung 2, Vision 2.

44. *Paradise Now*.
Rung 4, Rite 4. Breaking the touch barriers.

45. *Paradise Now.*
Nona Howard improvising,
actors and spectators entwined.

46. *Paradise Now.*
Rung 6, Rite 6. The "voyager"
and the opposing force.

47. *Paradise Now*.
Julian Beck in center.

47

48

"And you! What are _you_ doing to help Aida and Radames? Will you just sit there and let them die?"

The New Yorker   Dec. 14 1968

49. The troupe in a waiting room.

49

few exceptions, has become excessively frivolous; everything is idealized and unreal. The framework—velvet, lights, architecture, costumes—makes the spectator into a prince, which he is not. On the Establishment stage everything is perfect, even poverty. "Too much perfection on Broadway," Julian says, "and their delectable things shall not profit." The spectator is protected from everything, and then goes home to his personal miseries. "I am a man not interested in theatre," Julian wrote, "the entertainments that demean our being, the dissemination of lies. Fun is destructive while joy creates." Actors in the system cannot really contribute and create, for they are entirely dominated by the concerns of money and success.

Is it possible then to work in the theatre? Yes, but only by doing something different, by changing the actor-spectator relationship and doing it not by beginning with the traditional conception of the actor but by changing the actor in the first place. In order to change the world it is not enough that the actor mouth the words; he must be directly engaged in the attempt himself. In this connection, the Becks' attitude toward the Stanislavski "Method" in the United States calls for brief comment. Stanislavski's theories have been circulated often enough and need not be discussed here. What is not as widely known is that the American fixation on Stanislavski—the "Method"—is grounded in an exceedingly small segment of his total work, which he never completed. In adopting this segment to the last letter, the propagators of the "Method" treated it as if it were the sum total of Stanislavski's theories, even though as early as 1934 he cautioned his American emulators against the danger of misuse. Be that as it may, the Living Theatre reproaches the "Method" for its total reliance on rationality and psychology and upholds the premise that life unfolds on various, diverse levels that are intricately interconnected and also simultaneous. The Living Theatre, devoted as it is to changing the world, knows that change will not take place without some sort of "sanctification" (whether there is a god in the heaven of the audience or not). Accordingly, its objectives are secular, but they are shaped into forms appropriate to tradition, because tradition is, above all, union with a principle at the deepest level.

For Julian, in any event, changing the world is a duty. His conscience is grounded in Jewish religious creed according to which "the world is in the process of creation and it is man's sacred duty to assist God in this process."

As far back as the eviction from 14th Street, Julian announced to the press that the company would play in lobbies, in gyms, in the streets. In Italy, *Mysteries* was presented in courtyards and in the corridor of a university. More than ever, Julian was trying to shake off the shackles of theatrical structures and play in the streets.

The idea is to make the theatre a place of unification, a place without disguises, without subterfuges. All devices that are not essential must be done away with; what is essential, according to the Becks' interpretation of Artaud's concept, is the actor's body, his bodily presence, his acceptance as both victim and priest.

A few months after the introduction of *Mysteries*, Julian, writing about the work of the Living Theatre previous to the piece, characterized it, even at this early period, as an attempt to encourage the public to become once again what it was when the first dramatic works were created: "a congregation led by priests, a choral ecstasy of reading and response, dance, seeking transcendence, a way out and up, the vertical thrust." Approaching the theatre in this manner implies a relentless honesty—another key word to the Living Theatre—on the part of the actor. "Actors don't have to speak better than people. Nothing is better than people. We have to get rid of the idea that elocution constitutes good speech. I think elocution and the throaty way even our best actors often speak is related to some kind of respect for money. (. . .) I want actors to stop posing. I am talking to Method actors, too, to stop trying to create effects and to break through into the representation of honest life."[1]

Thus, the actor is stripped of his entire stock of instruments: mannerisms, cultivated voice, "bearing." The actors of the Living Theatre are "gauche," as Julian himself has put it, as a reaction against the actors of Establishment theatre—polite, "artistic," conventional. The theatre has debased itself over the centuries and must be "redeemed." . . .

Overall, the work of the Living Theatre is one of unification. It strives for unification in reuniting actor and spectator, in abolishing the distance between them both spatially and temporally. To this end, a language is needed, a language close to the gestic and vocal hieroglyphs of Artaud, in other words, symbols.

Initiation, the goal of which is deliverance and release, must be totally distinguished from the exclusively Western (and specifically Christian) mystical experience, the goal of which is salvation. The mystical experience is religious and exoteric. It is a departure from the self; an *ex-tasis*, not an internal realization. Mysticism is transitory.

Rites and symbols are the expressions of initiation. Initiation is not a religious phenomenon, for religion is intended for the masses whereas initiation is selective: the individual takes the initiative with a view to his spiritual development. It cannot be conducted by the individual in isolation; it implies a link to a traditional organization. A member of this organization exercises a spiritual and thus inexpressible influence upon the initiate, which influence becomes imprinted in him. Since the influence is inex-

[1] Julian Beck, "Thoughts on Theatre from Jail," *The New York Times,* February 21, 1965.

pressible, the initiation is secret. Initiation is the only private rite; public religious cults, for example, are unrestricted and thus readily comprehensible.

An organization is traditional when it is based upon a principle that radiates outward from the center to the circumference. All composites, all juxtapositions of diverse origins (theosophy, occultism, etc.) are profane (syncretic). They are counterfeits of traditional organizations.[2]

As for the term "sect," sometimes applied to the Living Theatre, it is meaningless. Without a mother religion to exalt, how can there be a sect?

The expression "total" theatre is also often bandied about. It is an inaccurate expression, calling forth as it does an image of a theatre that functions as a point of convergence for all other forms of art—a requirement satisfied only by Wagner's totalitary conception of the ideal theatre. (Even in Wagner's case, the *"Gesamtkunstwerk"* excluded spoken dialogue and ballet.)

Adherents of the contemporary "total" theatre envision spaces designed to undergo infinite varieties of transformations, equipped with every imaginable technical innovation; in total contrast, the Living Theatre refuses to admit any intermediary between actor and spectator, as demonstrated in its production of *Mysteries* and *Antigone*. Props have been banished and lighting is minimal; the only offerings, in symbolic fashion, are body and spirit.

In this respect, the Living Theatre is quite close to the conceptions of another contemporary innovator: Poland's celebrated Jerzy Grotowski. Both the Living Theatre and Grotowski's "laboratory" have opted for a "theatre of poverty"—a term often used by Grotowski—based primarily on the actor. Grotowski, however, restricts himself to working in vir-

[2] On these questions see René Alleau, *De la nature des symboles,* Flammarion, 1958; René Guénon, *Aperçus sur l'initiation,* Éditions traditionelles, Paris, 1953 (second edition).

tual privacy, for a small audience. He regards the stage as something of an operating table, an experimental laboratory, playing to about eighty spectators, the action unfolding both on the stage and in the auditorium or else in a severely limited irregular space, precisely determined in advance. Grotowski's actor is altogether different from the Living Theatre's, and the spectator is in effect a *voyeur* placed in a privileged position. For example, in Grotowski's *The Constant Prince*, a free adaptation from Calderon, the action takes place in an "arena" surrounded by high wood partitions and the spectator looks on from above. He sees an almost naked actor using his body as if it were a seismograph, registering torments and joys, inflicted on him by the other actors.

The Living Theatre has not adopted this approach to the actor-spectator relationship, because in the final analysis their goal is to secure the spectator's participation and through this involvement to effect change in the world. A spectator once made the following remark to Judith and Julian after a performance of *Antigone*: "When the troupe advanced toward the audience, toward the Argives, for final combat, I felt as if I had a weapon in my hands, as if we were going to kill each other. I was overcome by horror." Clearly, this was the ideal spectator for the Living Theatre; his attitude suggests that he was among those who have experienced violence in the performance as it is in the world and have the potential to contribute to the effort to change it. Violence does not always engender violence. It depends.

21

THE MAIDS

The Living Theatre was rehearsing *The Maids* at the time it introduced *Mysteries* in Paris in October, 1964. Genet wrote the play in prison, Judith prepared her staging instructions in prison, and Julian designed the sets and costumes in prison. The company began rehearsing it in Heist-sur-Mer, where Judith and Julian rejoined it after their release, and the premiere took place in Berlin on February 26, 1965.

Although the company now takes a detached view of this production, regarding it as belonging to its early phase, it was nevertheless quite enthusiastic about it at the time. Judith and Julian had been longing to do Genet for many years, and when they were in London they went to see Genet's agent, who had never heard about them before. As luck would have it, the telephone rang one day and it was Genet himself calling. He agreed right then and there to the Becks' doing any play of his they wished to do, because he thought highly of their work. For a while, the Becks were torn between *The Balcony* or *The Screens,* the latter never having been staged at the time; they finally settled on *The Maids.*

The Maids, Genet's second play, was published in 1948, two years after *Deathwatch.* It was inspired by a news item that had a great effect on the surrealists at the time. Two sisters, Léa and Christine Papin, brought up in a convent in Le Mans, were placed in a bourgeois household as maids by their mother. They were submissive and tolerated unreasonableness, insults, and admonishments. But, one fine day they seized their employers, mother and daughter, and in the words of the eminent psychiatrist Jacques Lacan, who wrote an account of the case in 1933, "They tore their victims' eyes out of their sockets while they were still alive—a deed said to be unprecedented in the annals of crime—and beat them to death. Then, making use of household items within reach, such as a hammer, a pewter jug, a kitchen knife, they set upon the bodies of their victims, crushing their faces, baring their sex organs. inflicting deep incisions in the thighs and buttocks of one and smearing the blood over the thighs of the other. Subsequently, they washed the instruments of the atrocious rite, cleaned themselves up, and went to sleep in the same bed."

Genet was not planning to write a play about a double murder, for it would have been conventional and, needless to say, unplayable. He had a grudge against Western theatre that was particularly acute at the time he was working on this play. He had just learned about the pageantry of Japanese, Chinese, and Balinese theater, which made Western theatre seem gross by comparison. He was dreaming of a form of art that would be a "deep entanglement of active symbols," as he put it. But a play in which all would be foreseeable would without doubt be badly received, beginning with the actors, cringing in their stupidity. So Genet depended on the exhibitionism of the actors, as he saw them. Eventually, he devised a play wherein the characters play a role, thereby acting as actors do. This acting is sanctified by the real suicide of one of the maids, the other probably faces the gallows, while Madame remains unharmed. The maids have suppressed only her representation, embodied in one of them. The other, who provokes and encourages the suicide, acquires the supreme grandeur of the criminal—a constantly recurring obsession of Genet's.

(Genet made a revealing comment in his preface to the French edition of *The Maids*: "I go to the theatre in order to see myself on the stage (in-

carnated by a single person or with the aid of a
multiple personage in the form of a story), in a form
in which I could not, or would not, dare to see or to
dream myself; knowing myself, however, to be such.")

The Living Theatre used the first version of the
play in Bernard Frechtman's translation; this is
somewhat different from the 1958 version, which was
republished in 1963. Critics often neglected to in-
form themselves on this point, and they were quick
to accuse the company of making changes in Genet's
text. I have indicated the principal differences between the two versions (but not the specifics of
plot) in the summary that follows. I, for one, find
the first version superior.

The play unfolds without intermission in a single setting, that of Madame's room, decorated in
Louis XV style. Madame is about to leave as the
play opens. In fact she is Claire, the maid, playing
Madame in her absence. She talks at great length
about her lover who is going to prison, as a result of
being doublecrossed; she is talking to "Claire," her
maid, who is acted out by Solange. At every opportunity, the sisters leave their appointed domain, the
kitchen with its smells and chores and the garret
they sleep in, and spend their time in Madame's
room—a place for pretty gestures, for primping, a
place with glitter, with jewels, clothes, flowers, with
many mirrors and a balcony for showing off. They
are playing at being Madame (who is twenty-five
years old) and her maid, as the clients of the whorehouse in *The Balcony* play at being bishops, admi-
rals, or newborn babes.

Solange is older than Claire by five years; she is
thirty-five. They are waiting for the real Madame,
who is going to come home in despair: her lover is
indeed in prison. Claire has caused his downfall with
an anonymous letter, but Madame is unaware of
that. To borrow an interesting insight of George
Bataille's, the sisters, who lack any "sovereignty" of

their own, seek an inverted sovereignty, such as criminals bestow on themselves.

The alarm clock rings, and the ceremony in Madame's room must end. Solange regrets not having had time to "finish off" Claire-Madame; one day, she nearly strangled Claire-Madame, for which Claire would have denounced her and followed her to prison, to form the sacred couple of criminal and saint.

The maids are preparing Madame's lime tea and decide to put poison in it. Monsieur has just telephoned; he has been freed and revenge is imminent. Claire ecstatically recites the exploits of great criminals, among them a nun's poisoning twenty-seven Arabs. Madame returns.

(*Second version.* Additions: Claire describes how she has written her letters of denunciation. Cuts: most importantly, Claire's recital of great criminal exploits.)

Madame declares herself ready to leave for Guiana if her lover is condemned to prison—and it is here that she reveals a profound likeness to the maids. They tell her at last that Monsieur has telephoned. Madame regains her composure and rushes off in a taxi without having drunk her tea. First, she has repaired her makeup, however, and asked for Claire's advice on her hairdo, displaying the sort of intimacy that nearly always prevails between women.

(*Second version.* Additions: a lengthy account by Madame on Monsieur's arrest; a dialogue between her and the maids on the subject of her wardrobe, which is as sacred to the sisters as the chapel of the Virgin Mary. Cuts: the long passage where Madame expresses her delight over the good news and asks Claire's help with her hair while Claire is making vain efforts to have her drink her tea.)

The maids are alone again. Solange betrays a determination that frightens Claire a little bit. To gain time, Claire suggests that they be more careful;

they might be overheard or taken by surprise; the room itself records their movements. Claire would like it if she and her sister said a prayer, at least. Useless, Solange says. God is already listening. The walls are his ears. Claire puts on Madame's white robe.

(*Second version.* Surprisingly, the whole passage is replaced by a bitter monologue by Claire on Madame's "kindness" and by a dialogue in which the maids reproach themselves in a tasteless manner for having failed with their tea plot; Claire becomes Madame abruptly, without putting on the robe.)

Solange, again very determined, asks Claire to go through the customary formalities they have been observing at the beginning of the ceremony. Claire, having put on the white robe over her own black one, comes in and imperiously asks Solange to insult her. Solange is astonished, then seizes a whip and rushes upon Claire. But Claire-Madame is exhausted; if only they could conclude the ceremony and go to bed! Solange consents at last to speak to Claire as Claire and takes her to the kitchen. She tells her that she knows a way to "put an end to all suffering." The stage remains empty for a moment; the breeze blows open the window.

(*Second version.* The long illustration of Claire's "cowardice" is sustained in a series of curt replies. The effect of exasperation and fatigue is sharply diminished, the whip is cut, and Solange's role is substantially reduced. She does not take Claire to the kitchen, but steps on her and pushes her in a corner where she remains collapsed.)

Solange delivers an immense monologue, declaring that Claire-Madame is dead at last, strangled by the gloves used by the maids for washing dishes. Solange has become somebody: "Madame and Monsieur will call me Mademoiselle Solange Lemercier." She imitates Madame wearing mourning for Claire, then resumes her identity and pretends to answer the questions of the police chief. She is glorious, she is

Solange who "strangled her sister." She recalls humiliations endured, she imagines herself mounting the steps to the gallows, then delights in an imaginary account of Claire's funeral, with all the domestics in the procession. Now, Solange is part of the world of outcasts, like the police. At this moment, Claire enters wearing the white robe. Solange sees her and her voice falters.

(*Second version.* Sharply abbreviated. The monologue is nevertheless a hundred lines. Claire remains slouched in the corner.)

Claire, speaking in Madame's voice, demands her tea and behaves in an altogether ruthless manner: "We are alone in the world," she tells Solange. "Nothing exists but the altar on which one of the sisters is about to sacrifice herself." All Solange has to do now is to prevent her from changing her mind; she wants to end the game but Claire is pushing her toward another goal. She is repeating Claire's words: "Madame will take her tea. . . . Now she must go to sleep. . . . I will watch her. . . ." Claire drinks the tea lying on Madame's bed, and dies. Solange has a monologue: She imagines a party given by the "real" Madame, the orchestra, the elegance, Monsieur's endearments, lovers. . . . But Madame is dead. "Her two maids are alive; they burst out of Madame's rigid body, deservedly free. . . . We are beautiful, gay, drunk, and free!"

(*Second version.* Here again, Genet abbreviated the scene drastically. It is all of three pages. The references to the altar and to the sacrifice are gone, the lyrical, dramatic crescendo, the tension, are reduced to a bare skeleton, and Solange's final monologue is deleted.)

22

THREE MEN, NOT THREE PRETTY BOYS. . . .

It is not surprising that you should want to stage
The Maids. As Daniel Guérin has noted, "The
anarchist's permanent state of revolt leads him to
experience sympathy for the 'irregulars,' for those
outside the law, and to embrace the cause of the
convict, condemned by everyone else." What exactly
was the point you attempted to make by having
male actors take the roles?

JULIAN: Judith and I saw the play in New York
in 1949, I think. It was a very interesting production
and we thought the play was fantastic. The version
we used is the first one, it is much more revolutionary than the other; the dimensions of madness
and ritual had been sharply reduced by Genet. An
actor or a director perhaps told Genet that the play
was not logical enough, not "well-made." I don't
know . . .

JUDITH: In New York, the parts were played
by three women. We started rehearsing it with three
girls, but it all seemed wrong to me pretty soon. The
play remained rigidly fixed to its psychology; all we
had was a situation with three hysterical women.
Genet himself would have liked to have seen it performed by three pretty boys, but we decided on a
different course. Our three actors didn't have the
physique of pretty boys, they were not effeminate.
They had broad shoulders. Accordingly, homosex-
uality was not the primary factor, as it would have
been with pretty boys. You saw three men dressed
as women, yet they were three average men. It was
much more embarrassing to see men as slaves, slaves
of a "woman" who herself was the slave of a system

that includes the two maids. The spectator couldn't cling to some such comforting interpretation as "these are homosexuals—or homosexuals playing homosexuals playing *The Maids*." This was very uncomfortable for the audience, because the three men conveyed the idea of a total degradation, even if the matter was never stated.[1] This was clearly much worse, in the final analysis. The play is psychological when it is performed by women, but it takes on a predominantly social character when played by men.

What about the set and the costumes?

JULIAN: With the help of Jim Tiroff, who is a member of the troupe, we turned the stage into a veritable temple of human enslavement. The altar Claire alludes to, everything was black and white or metallic. We devised Greek columns draped out of white velvet; it was very ingenious. The furnishings, the screen, the bed, the dressing table, the chandelier, all these were made by Jim Tiroff out of old bicycle wheels, curtain rods, metal beds, and various iron structures. It was all extraordinarily chic and glittering. And gladioli everywhere, as Genet wanted it. The maids were dressed in black, a sort of shiny satin, with white cuffs and collars. Very sado-masochistic. Their stockings and their laced shoes were black, highly polished. Madame also wore black; first we used fur for her costume, then we did it over in a very pretty black fabric. The maids and Madame are alike. . . . They wore wigs. . . . As in classic plays, there was an entrance for nobility—on the right, behind the bed—and one for the lower classes—on the left, behind the dressing table, leading to the kitchen. The entrance in the center is reserved for the gods; it is the window and

[1] The play should by no means be looked upon as a plea in behalf of the social class of domestics. Genet himself objected to all cut-and-dried interpretations. "I imagine that there is a union of domestics," he noted in his preface to the French edition, "but I am not concerned with that."

the balcony where Claire struts at night. The window is for God to enter. We put a white curtain across it which stirs gently when God enters to listen to the sisters. The window opens and we put behind it a big black box and pierced it in a lot of spots: God enters and the stars shine.

This elegance makes the play seem far removed from the other European productions of the Living Theatre. . . .

JULIAN: It was definitely the most "old-fashioned" one of all. If it were to be done over again, it is the interpretation—on the physical level, above all—that would be changed. But, I am quite sure that it was the most "beautiful" production that we have ever mounted. The costumes were so "feminine," so elegant, and everything had such a dazzling chic and luxury about it. And all that in a setting of velvet and metal. . . .

(It ought to be noted here that Judith thinks that *The Spook Sonata,* staged in 1954, was their most "beautiful" production.)

23

THE DISTANT ORIGINS OF FRANKENSTEIN

Judith had been attracted to the Frankenstein theme for many years, but the company had never had sufficient time and money to undertake a project based on it. Judith and Julian, along with several members of the troupe, had been researching the subject whenever time permitted. One of the most fruitful sources proved to be movies, ranging from the very old to the contemporary: the *Frankenstein* series, Fritz Lang's *Metropolis,* the films of Murnau, Chaplin's *Modern Times.* Little by little, a picture collection had been assembled. In due course, after a great deal of research had been completed, the company also used Mary Shelley's admirable if imperfect novel—the original source of the Frankenstein literature. (At the Venice festival, which is dedicated to prose theatre, the management insisted that the Living Theatre furnish textual references for the program notes. That was the only reason that the company undertook to provide information on literary sources.)

The return to Mary Shelley was beneficial. In fact, the novel's most conspicuous contribution to the play consists of a superb monologue expressing anarchist ideas that certainly did not originate with the Living Theatre. Mary Shelley was the daughter of an active feminist, Mary Wollstonecraft, and the anarchist theoretician, and propagator of non-violence, William Godwin. The play's philosophical foundation is embedded in the idea that the world must be changed, that a new man must evolve, and all human suffering must be eliminated. The motives of Dr. Frankenstein are to be found in that idea. In the novel, Frankenstein is driven principally by a passionate curiosity about the mysteries of life. Still, the profession of faith in anarchist values is clearly there, and it is not surprising that the Living Theatre should utilize the most anarchist part of the book in preference to others.

Frankenstein himself was created under interesting circumstances. Byron, Shelley, and his wife were spending some time at Lake Geneva in Switzerland in 1816. In a library in Geneva they came upon a collection labeled "Fantasmagoriana." The evenings were long, and the three decided that each should write a Gothic tale to while away the time. Shelley gave up on it quickly. Byron wrote *"Vampire,"* which was to be completed, signed, and published by his companion, Polidori. Mary wrote *Frankenstein, or the Modern Prometheus,* which was to be published in London in 1818.

In the novel Victor Frankenstein is a young, brilliant scientist from Geneva, educated at German universities. The time is the end of the eighteenth century. At Ingolstadt, he succeeds in constructing a creature of repulsive physical aspect but normal brain, out of organs taken from dead bodies. The ancient curse pronounced on all imitators of the Creator is going to strike him down. When Frankenstein sees his creature stir for the first time, he is terrified by what he has done and flees. A letter from his father brings the news that his little brother William was strangled in Geneva on the Plaine of Plainpalais (at that time outside the walls of the city). A medallion worn by William is found in the pocket of a young girl, Justine Moritz, and she perishes on the gallows. Wandering about in a stunned state, Frankenstein stumbles into a valley near the Mont Blanc when someone, moving at a prodigious pace despite the ice, overtakes him. It is the Creature, who has built himself a hut in this desolate place. He recounts everything that happened to him from the time Frankenstein fled the labora-

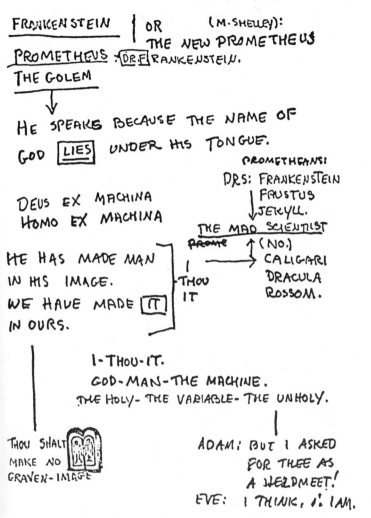

From Judith Malina's notes for *Frankenstein*.

tory. His account takes up some thirty pages: the discovery of sensations, his first contacts with people who harshly repulse him, a vision of idyllic happiness with a family united by most tender love, his expulsion by the same family, his rescue of a drowning young girl, repaid by being shot at. Not knowing where to go, the Creature sets out toward Geneva bearing eternal hatred for mankind, which has turned him into an evil being. A boy enters his hiding place; it is William. The Creature kills him and puts his medallion in the pocket of a sleeping girl, as an act of revenge against humanity.

At the end of his account, the Creature asks Frankenstein to create a companion for him, because he aspires to happiness. If he is not to be permitted to love, if he is not to be provided with an object he would be able to love, then he will devote himself to an unrelenting hatred of humans. Frankenstein accepts the task on condition that the couple-to-be stay away from inhabited land forever. He then departs for Scotland. He all but completes the work, but destroys it in a sudden bout of rage. The Creature arrives to conclude the bargain, only to be disappointed, whereupon he warns Frankenstein that he will be present at his wedding. Later on, the body of Frankenstein's friend is found strangled on the beach. He returns to Geneva to marry an orphan girl chosen for him by his father; on the evening of the wedding, he finds her lying on the bed, pale as ashes. The Creature has kept his promise. Frankenstein decides to destroy his creation and pursues him to the far north. During the pursuit, in a state of total exhaustion, he is rescued by a boat. He dies on board. The captain discovers the Creature leaning over Frankenstein's body. "Sullied by crimes, torn by remorse, where can I find repose outside death?" the Creature exclaims in despair and then resolves to immolate himself on a pyre he himself will build. An ice floe carries him off into the darkness.

The Living Theatre's production, created by the company in community and put in final focus by Judith and Julian, was presented a few months after *The Maids*. It ranged over a great many supplementary themes, having drawn inspiration from wherever it could be found.

24

FRANKENSTEIN, ACT I:
Birth of the Creature

The final version of *Frankenstein* is considerably different from the one presented at the Venice festival in October, 1965. The production then had not yet reached the stage of structuring the company had been aiming at. In November the Venice version was presented in Berlin, but there were only three performances given, the same number as in Venice. During the next nine months, *Frankenstein* was not presented at all; then, in August, 1966, a new version, which had been prepared during a stay in Reggio-Emilia, Italy, was unveiled at the Cassis festival. In all, there were a mere fifty-one European performances of both versions of the play. None has satisfied the Living Theatre so far.

A description of each of the three acts, the way they were being performed in 1969 follows; at the end of each act, the principal changes in comparison to previous versions are sketched out, together with such critical comments as may be relevant.

The action takes place inside and in front of a three-story-high rectangular metal structure, equipped with gangplanks and ladders. Vertical metal tubing divides the area into fifteen equal compartments. On the ground level, the compartments are designated A1, A2, A3, etc., from left to right; on the second level, B1, B2, B3, etc.; and on the third, C1, C2, C3, etc. [See photo insert.] Each actor plays a number of roles, except the one playing Frankenstein (Bill Shari in Cassis and Venice, Julian everywhere else). Most of the roles were invented by the actors playing them.

The reader must be cautioned that an integrated, detailed exegesis of each component in what is essentially a gigantic, irrational spectacle is not possible for the spectator, however well-informed he might be. If the space devoted here to the *Frankenstein* production appears to be inordinately disproportionate, justification is based on those two reasons alone.

Act I. Levitation: Silence. Fifteen actors face the audience, all of them seated Indian-style. A girl in B5 speaks into a microphone in a slow, expressionless voice, informing the audience every five minutes or so that the people on stage are engaged in meditation, the purpose of which is to levitate the girl seated in center. This control booth is a representation of a world where everyone is keeping watch on everyone else; in the third act the entire structure will become a prison and B5 will become the lodging of prison guards. The commentaries are delivered in several languages (German, English, Italian, Spanish, French). The actors wear their everyday clothes, but not their brightest ones, and provide such accessories as might be required.

After about twenty minutes, the voice announces that the final phase of meditation is about to begin in the form of yoga breathing, which has healing powers; at its conclusion, the girl is going to levitate. The program informs the audience that if the levitation succeeds, the play will end then and there. (The breathing exercise consists in saying the word *Puraka* in one's mind when the air reaches the lungs, then repeating the word *Kumbhaka* four times while retaining the air in the lungs—inadvisable to those untrained in the art—then saying the word *Rechaka* twice while exhaling. The words are to be said in the mind only throughout the exercise.) The Living Theatre firmly believes that one day, "if the concentration is intense enough and the purity of the participants deep enough," the levitation will occur.[1] The spectator awaits the impossible.

Victimization: The levitation has failed. All eyes turn menacingly toward the girl in the center (Mary Mary). Failure is due to inadequate concentration by the participants, yet there must be a victim.[2] She tries to escape, she cries out, but the others drive her back. She is trapped like a wild beast, and a strongly knotted net is thrown over her. She is then placed in a coffin of black wood. The cries of the living dead penetrate through the coffin to the spectators' ears.

Hoisted upon the backs of the actors, the coffin is carried down the aisle among the spectators. Two veiled women follow the procession, with a thoughtful Frankenstein at the end of the line. Those in the procession emit mournful sounds to the beat of hand striking against thigh. The coffin is carried back to the stage and placed sideways in A3. (A2 and A4 are kept dark in the back to allow for costume changes.)

The No!: When the procession is formed, an actor cries out "No!" and flees into the auditorium. It is a positive "No," addressed to oppression, because he recognizes the guilt of the group for the

---

[1] The Living Theatre follows the tenets of Raja-Yoga, according to which "one discovers, without seeking them, yet even more in seeking them, the powers of the occult (*siddhis*). Some of these powers, such as clairvoyance or clairaudience, the healing of certain diseases, or the reading of the thoughts of others, appear early in the practice of *dharana*. Others, like levitation, appear much later. . . . Whether these miraculous powers exist, or whether they are the fruits of overheated imagination, is very difficult to determine, for the true Yogi will not condescend to exhibit them for selfish ends or to demonstrate them for the benefit of the curious." (Translated from: Jean Herbert, *Spiritualité Hindoue*, Albin Michel, 1947.)

[2] As Julian says, the crowd kills the hero if he disappoints them.

failure of the levitation. The others search for the fugitive, directed by two actors using walkie-talkies with the controlled calm of policemen. To have said "No" to the law that permitted the extermination of the girl who could not levitate is to be automatically designated as victim. The actor is captured and hanged in B3. Another actor, witnessing the scene,

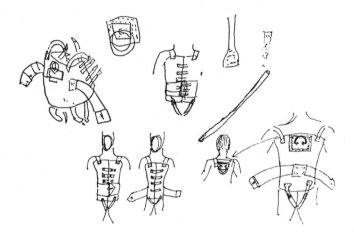

Julian Beck's preliminary sketches for a secure hanging in *Frankenstein.*

says "No" to the hanging, whereupon he himself is captured and executed. And so on, one by one. Each execution illustrates a particular form of corporal punishment: hanging, then gas chamber (B2), quartering (A5), beheading (C2), crucifixion (A2), bullets (stage front), electric chair (B4), iron maiden (A1), garrote (A4), firing squad (A4-A5), guillotine (C4). The executions, although very dramatic, are not performed naturalistically: the executioner has no ax, for example, but mimes the gesture, whereupon the block drops down, not the head. The executioners, in turn, become victims themselves. The lights, which have been focusing on each execution, compartment by compartment, now pick out

Frankenstein sitting on the coffin in profound con-
templation. There are only two other survivors.

Shadow Play: Frankenstein chalks on the coffin
in Hebrew the words, "The dead shall be raised." A
screen descends in front of the coffin. A lamp etches
Frankenstein's silhouette as he opens the coffin, raises
the body's arm, holding it by its shriveled fingers,
makes an incision with a lancet, connects a network
of tubing attached to the ceiling for pumping blood,
removes the heart and places it in a glass jar.

Service for the Dead: Meanwhile, the two survivors have been removing the bodies one by one,
with the deliberate slowness of professionals. In C2,
a priest is saying the Catholic service for the dead
(*"et exspecto resurrectionem mortuorum"*) over the
victim of the beheading, while in C4, facing a bugler
playing taps, a military chaplain is delivering a prayer
for the victim of the guillotine ("the dead shall be
raised").[3] The voice in B5 repeats the prayer in
various languages, including Hebrew, in a solemn
tone.

An old man and woman have been laboriously
making their way across the stage, through the
corpses. The old man has a hammer in his hand and
is tapping it against the vertical tubes built into the
structure along the way. (For the spectator, this is
probably the most difficult image to interpret in the
entire play. Judith's notes explain it in the following
terms: "the poor and the old: they are clochards
[vagrants], they are also elemental. They do work,
but they are bent down by it. They are burdened.
The image is from *Anna Karenina,* of the old one
striking the railroad rails, bent down, mysterious,
covered with snow. They also are, as in *Anna Karenina,* oracular. They work below the social structure,
but it is they who move it. The *Lumpenproletariat.*

---

[3] From the Prayer Book for Jews in the Armed
Forces of the United States. The priest represents the
burial by the Church, the military chaplain the burial by
the State.

They are the poorest of the poor, but he has the lamp and the tool, and in her bag is foot, brain, eye and the prophecy. The old man is wearing a coat and hat, and the old woman is shaking a stick to which strips of white paper are attached by threads over his head throughout their journey.

The screen is lifted. The corpse lies in the center of the stage, lit from above. Two veiled women undress it, as in the descent from the cross, leaving only a cloth to cover the sexual organs. They hand paint brushes to Frankenstein, and he chalks a magic circle and traces mysterious signs on the chest, sides, and thighs.

Automation-Collage: On C level, an actor who seems to be a fugitive from Chaplin's *Modern Times* is executing a series of mechanical gestures. Three others, also in C, wave portraits of Marx and Lenin along with a placard reading "To each/his need/from each/his power." They march on the narrow gangplanks while declaiming Marxist maxims in jerky, broken tones of voice. From the control booth in B5, an actor wrapped in a black hood is introduced as the spokesman of "international industries," and proceeds to read in monotones, amplified by loudspeakers, capitalist slogans consisting of typical phrases taken from books on economics. (The texts recited in this scene have been arranged as a collage. Besides Mao and Whitman, passages have been drawn from *The Age of Automation* by Sir Leon Bargrit and Bertrand Russell's *Power*. The total effect is that of an unmilitant discussion among electronic machines, each being given equal importance. On the other hand, the voice at the control booth explains that automation will provide an altogether higher level of civilization.)

How to End Human Suffering: Frankenstein, his back to the audience, is terrified and trembling as he observes the tumult and unrest that has taken hold of the occupants of the structure, which has become a representation of the world. He reproduces the gestures, taken in by the movement, for a moment. Then he illuminates the structure with the lamp he has been holding and inquires in a sorrowful voice, "How can we end human suffering?" All movement stops, the lights go out. A brief and total silence ensues. Four times Frankenstein repeats his question, which will be the key motif of all action to come. He addresses it to the capitalist, to the mechanical worker, to the Marxists, and finally to the old man and woman, who provide the answer. Each question is asked twice, first while the tumult is still going on, then when everything has stopped and the light is off. Then Frankenstein uses his flashlight.

The downtrodden, who are the real source of power—as they might be, in their terror, in Genet's *The Maids,* or in *Metropolis*—the exploited, respond. The old woman removes a "foot" (a constructed prop that fits over the corpse-actor's foot) from her sack, while saying "Fooooooooot." She places it over the foot on the corpse. She does the same with the brain (a skullcap), and the eye, which is placed on the navel and emits a red glow.

The old woman (Jenny Hecht) is crouched by the corpse like a sorceress, and in a shrill voice she pronounces a prophecy in the form of a riddle to Frankenstein. The prophecy consists of a poem written by Julian: "Human suffering need not be / When you master three times three / Stand the body on its brain / Watered with electric rain / Electric eye and brain and feet / Are all you need to make real meat / Pharaoh's slaves built tomb and wall / Newton's apple need not fall / These body organs from the grave / Are all you need to make a slave." Then a flash projector lights up the corpse, which is now held upside down as if it was the cross of St. Peter by the couple, as in a black mass.

In A5 and C5, immediately below and above the capitalist, are portraits of Mao and of Walt Whitman; the actors in these compartments are reciting martial poems by the two.

Construction of the Laboratory: From now on, the impetus is clear. Frankenstein is promoted to head a government project, thus going from magic and necromancy into official science. He constructs a laboratory attached to the structure on the left of the stage. It is built of metal tubing by workers who display the same mechanical gestures as in the preceding scene. The laboratory is pentagonal, containing an elevated platform with an operating table that slopes in the direction of the audience, with the corpse on it. A light flashes on A3 to show the Golem—a mythological monster antedating Mary Shelley's by several centuries—in the process of killing three rabbis. Frankenstein and his assistants don the white gowns and masks worn by doctors, and the operation begins. One hears the customary "Yes, doctor" being repeated. Instruments are passed to the surgeon. Luminous panels on C exhibit anatomical slides. The heart stops. Frankenstein and his assistants go into the structure to get another heart, that of the victim of electrocution: electricity, which was the instrument of death earlier, now returns as the instrument of life. (This idea and its variations have frequently appeared in Living Theatre productions, for example in *The Connection.*)

Paracelsus, Freud, Wiener: The Creature is not yet alive. The phantoms of the three great personages come to Frankenstein's aid. They appear in C5, masked, one after the other. The first among them is Paracelsus, a forerunner of modern medicine. (In Mary Shelley's novel, Victor Frankenstein is a keen student of Paracelsus.) He instructs Frankenstein that the pineal gland is the seat of the soul and of the fundamental life impulse. The whole scene, abbreviated and a fakely serious treatise on the history of medicine, is relayed through a loudspeaker in B5, the voice serving as translator and annotator. Freud, in his turn, locates the life impulse in the sexual organs. Norbert Wiener informs him that electrical impulses are as manifest in the human mechanism as they are in electrical machinery, and that it is necessary to connect the electrodes to a cyclotron. The new heart begins to beat.

Long plastic tubes equipped with interior lights are now attached to the bodies of the executed victims inside the structure, connected to the laboratory. "Turn the creature on," Frankenstein orders, following Wiener's advice. And then, it is as if the creature in the laboratory were reproducing itself on the scale of Gulliver throughout the structure's three levels. Slowly, with a sort of whistling of lungs, reminding one of some mythical beast or sounds such as might be produced by a machine in another world, the dead begin to detach themselves from the faintly lit ground, and create in Chinese shadow silhouette the effect of a three-stories monster with red eyes. The curtain slowly descends. . . .

Notes to Act I: The first act lasts approximately one hour, the entire play two-and-a-half to three hours. In Cassis, the first act lasted two hours, the entire play five! Considerable changes have been made in the first act since Venice, affecting the line of general development. In Venice, the play contained a great deal of dialogue, which is no longer the case. In Venice, Frankenstein's assistants were two deformed creatures, Igor and Boris, and a woman, Bella. A hanged man who survived because the rope broke became Frankenstein's right-hand man, Fritz; he would later bring his master a sackful of bloody bits of flesh. After the executions, one heard the opening monologue from *Faust* recited in German. Paracelsus led Frankenstein to the cave of the oracle, having first delivered a passage from *De vita longa* in Latin. The oracle—the wizard of Endor—was questioned by Freud and Wiener, who also went along, but only Frankenstein was able to obtain a reply when he asked the wizard about the secret of life: Eye, tooth, foot, and electricity were the only ingredients needed to create real flesh. Helped by his assistants and the three scientists, Frankenstein assembled the parts, and the act ended the same way as it does now.

Frankenstein was staged and rehearsed in a number of theatres in Berlin, because no single one was available for any length of time. Rehearsals continued during the tours through Germany and Italy, wherever possible, even in hotel rooms, which accounts also for the inconsistencies and alterations.

Comments on Act I: It goes without saying that the symbolism of the first act is more complex than these few comments indicate. The play begins with a backward countdown ending in zero at the moment the levitation is supposed to take place. The world is a void. Frankenstein, an impotent spectator of violence and injustice, decides to start all over again from the beginning, in order to make the world different, more livable. All his actions, which come from a sincere desire to do good, take a wrong turn. He is creating evil against his own wishes. He seeks solutions where there are none. He should have started with what is—with the living, not the dead. His actions are aimed at raising his fellow-beings to a higher level, but in the course of the play they produce the same sort of victimization that was engendered at the attempt at levitation in the beginning; that, too, was a refusal of the world and of the possibilities of peacefully influencing the destiny of man. The refusal to believe in man as he is—evil but perfectible—is Frankenstein's "sin," and it becomes aggravated when he accepts service to the state. In the final analysis, he is not concerned with the living. (It goes without saying that the symbolism is more complex and these lines do not fully reveal the significance of the first act.)

25

FRANKENSTEIN, ACT II:
The Discovery of the
World As It Is

The Awakening of the Head: It is dark. The actors switch on flashlights on all three levels of the structure, creating a luminous poem. Red flashes first, then green, red again, and finally the arms and hands of the actors remain illuminated.

In the laboratory a blue phosphorescent light shines against a background of white walls. The corpse is always there, but now the actor is black—the first corpse's "double." The black actor is covered with phosphorescent plastic sheets reproducing muscles and bones. This skin is taken off while the mummy is unraveled.

He is opening his eyes! It is coming to life, gradually. It stirs frequently during the act, physically manifesting the transformations that are being represented in the structure, which is now an enlargement of the Creature's mind.

The ground floor of the structure is lit up. Actors, stripped to the waist, are slowly unraveling an upright mummy. It is the Ego. Once free of its swathes it touches its liberators, who convey in pantomime the idea of its movement. Then the Ego moves through the upper levels, which light up in its wake, to make the acquaintance of the actors there who represent the faculties of the mind.

The moment the Ego begins its journey through the structure to its appointed place on C, a network of plastic tubes, equipped with lights on the inside, is switched on and delineates in profile the contour of a giant head spreading through all three levels. The same head is printed on the blue-gray back curtain, accompanied by an English-language commentary describing the various functions of the mind. From left to right on level A: Animal Instincts, Subconscious, the Erotic; on level B: Intuition, Vision, Imagination, the Creative, Love; on level C: the forehead, containing Death (the coffin), the Ego, Wisdom, Knowledge. The actors who physically interpret these functions convey them through the use of an essential characteristic: Animal Instincts are characterized by force and bestiality; they are crude and unpredictable. The Subconscious interrogates; it is dangerous, suggestive, evasive, secretive. The Erotic is physical, mobile, changeable. Love embraces all who pass by; it is the redemptive, tranquilizing self. The Creative is mercurial and considerate—the miraculous self. It finds the answers and makes things function together. Imagination, like Intuition, is far-reaching, Intuition being the "projective" self, a sort of destiny in itself. Vision, by definition absorbing, seeks light unceasingly. Death, the destructive self, is the reminder of the end of everything (the coffin is "there"). The Ego is the manifest self: I am I, affirming the positive self. Wisdom seeks light, ever more keenly than Vision. Knowledge is rapacious and orderly.

(This poetic representation of the awakening of faculties beginning to exercise their powers does not aspire to scientific validity, of course, any more than did the operation performed on the Creature in the first act. The emphasis is not on up-to-date methods of surgery but on the "fabulous," on the moral significance inherent in the play.)

The Dream: The light changes to blue-green. "He is sleeping peacefully now, Doctor." The projection of the components of the mind has disappeared, but the actors remain where they have been, on all three levels of the structure, and mime the motions of passengers on a ship on the high seas, as in a slow motion film. They are on the first voyage of the mind. The roles are not assigned at random. On level A, the Animal Instincts become stokers, the

Subconscious turns into a look-out, the Erotic divides into sailors who save the women in a disaster. On level B, Intuition and Love are passengers, Vision is a look-out, the Creative and Imagination are sailors. On level C, the coffin becomes a lifeboat from which Death (the victim of the first act) will make its escape after the shipwreck, the Ego is a traveler, Wisdom is the captain of the ship, Knowledge or memory the radio operator.

The actors imitate the sound of the wind, the waves, the Morse code, the cries of the look-outs, the orders of the captain. It is announced that the ship has run into an iceberg. Everyone is on his own to save himself. While nets were quietly lowered from B to A in the former scene, the men now sit on the coffin and begin to row. Death escapes, the men fall into the sea by sliding down the tubing to A. Lying down on their backs, the actors turn into waves, moving their erect arms in patterns of an image that will be seen again in *Antigone.*

A choir of sirens in A3 intones the "Ode to Joy": Ariel's song from Shakespeare's *The Tempest,* sung to a passage from Beethoven's *Ninth Symphony,* a hymn to life, a celebration of the sea that transforms the body of the drowned into coral and pearl: "Full fathom five thy father lies; / Of his bones are coral made; / Those are pearls that were his eyes: / Nothing of him that doth fade, / But doth suffer a sea-change / into something rich and strange. / Sea-nymphs hourly ring his knell: / Hark! now I hear them—Ding dong bell." The actors repeat "ding dong bell" in a sonorous deep voice, as if produced by a gong. The Sirens repeat it, with a higher voice. "He is still sleeping peacefully, doctor," says an aid and another luminous visual poem, achieved with green lights only, closes the scene. The aid remarks that the Creature seems to wake up.

Icarus ("Levitation II"): A girl in B5, seated behind a desk as the one in Act I, reads news items taken at random from an English-language newspaper of the day of the performance into a microphone. She stops each time an actor inside the "mind" says something, then continues reading a new item without finishing the one that was interrupted. The news reader reflects the world we live in, current affairs, while across from her the Creature is going to rediscover the primitive myths of human passions, of human love and power, all of which are implicit in the news being read by the girl. The Creature conveys the myths of ancient Crete in pantomime.

Once again, the parts are distributed analogically. Wisdom, who was captain of the ship, changes into Icarus, and then into Buddha; Love becomes Pasiphae; Imagination turns into Theseus; the Animal Instincts into Zeus disguised as a bull and as the Minotaur; Intuition into Ariadne. Others are transposed by the same pattern of analogy.

On level B we see Daedalus, the great inventor who discovered the secret of flight. In a way, he is a precursor of Frankenstein, for he, too, seeks to escape the human condition. His son, Icarus, is now asking him to be taught the art of flying. Icarus climbs to C3 and practices the movement of wings with his arms. In A4, Zeus, wearing a mask of iron wires bearing the contours of a bull's head (as the mask in Cocteau's film, *The Blood of a Poet*), announces that he is going to swim to Crete and seduce Europa. He does so. Ariadne warns Europa: "Be careful, Europa!" The whole scene has a freshness and a delicious humor about it. Zeus returns to A4 with Europa on his back. Above, Pasiphae asks Daedalus for advice: How does one gain Zeus's love? By disguising oneself as a white cow, comes the answer. Zeus is seduced, he seduces. Her legs spread apart, Pasiphae gives birth to the Minotaur, who has climbed the ladder between A and B and simply popped up between Pasiphae's legs. He has the head of a bull and the body of a man; now he decides to ravage Crete. Daedalus invents the laby-

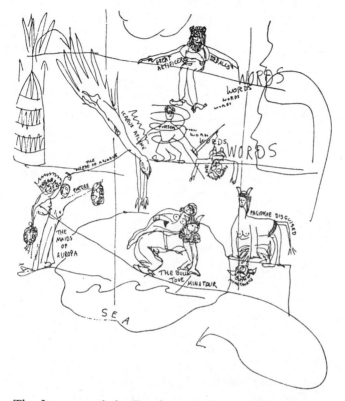

The Icarus myth in *Frankenstein* in a condensed sketch by Judith Malina.

rinth, represented by a roll of light paper tangled around the tubing on level B. The Minotaur is devouring his victims. Theseus appears, having found his bearings in the labyrinth with the help of red paper he obtained from Ariadne. He slays the Minotaur. Icarus slides down the tubing from C to A and is crushed on the ground. Blackout.

The Legend of Buddha: Frankenstein himself is going to provide the Creature with intellectual polish; it will translate it, in its own very primitive way, into The Legend of Buddha. Frankenstein is seated in A1, an elaborate set of earphones attached to his head. The Creature is wearing the same equipment in the laboratory. Reading from cards, which he draws and turns over one by one at an unvarying pace, he enunciates about a hundred words, each consisting of twelve letters, in a voice that places equal emphasis on every one. The choice of twelve-letter words (which are drawn from the preface of *The Anarchists* by I. L. Horowitz—these are the first ten: particularly, anthropology, introduction, disobedience, civilization, sociological, dysfunctions, organization, manipulation, impressively) allows for frequent use of those with Greek or Latin roots, which creates an impression of pseudoscientific, dry learning—especially when they are intoned the way Frankenstein intones them.

True betterment is spiritual, not intellectual, and decidedly not pseudointellectual. What the Creature is experiencing in his mind is one of the most famous instances of spiritual adventure, that of Buddha.

In A3, a group of Hindus in tattered garb circle in clockwise direction. The scene is bathed in golden light as they lament and wail. Above them, Prince Gautama (Siddhartha) and his bride Yasodhara, regally attired, circle in the opposite direction, absorbed in the delights of love. A ragged man leaves the circle below and raises his head toward Gautama. Yasodhara conceals the unhappiness of the poor man from Gautama's eyes with her veils. A young woman leaves the circle and dies. They take her body and place it in the center of the circle. Gautama sees it and decides to descend among the people. He crouches, executes a flip, and lands in the center of the circle, his legs crossed Indian-style. Renouncing all passions that engender suffering forever after, he climbs up the center pole to C3, where he becomes Buddha and assumes Buddha's position. A few of those in the circle succeed in hoisting themselves to B3, where they begin to meditate, becoming *bodhisatvas*; the others below continue their lamentation.

The legend of Buddha sketched by Judith Malina.

Blackout. Three flashes light up the recumbent actors, revealing among them in the shape of the Four Horsemen of the Apocalypse: War in A3, Plague in B4, Famine in B2, and Death (the victim in Act I) in C3. Four actors, their crouched backs covered by a cape and the first holding up an emblem of a horse's head, effect a rhythmic gallop in place. This image establishes the tone of what is to follow: the Creature is preparing to inflict death for the first time. Having been trained, he is going to enter the world, suffer rejection, and mete out a cruel revenge.

The Creature Speaks: The Creature removes the bonds that tie it to the operating table. It disappears. Upheaval in the interior of the head (the structure). The functions of the mind expel the Ego (Steve Ben Israel) into the world. From now on, the Ego is going to represent the Creature. At first, the rest of the stage is dark, the lights focus on the Ego; it is naked to the waist, and is trying painfully to express itself. Some indistinct sounds are heard, pronounced by Knowledge in C4. These are taken up by all the inhabitants of the structure, and they succeed in forming the first syllable: "It." The Creature on the stage pronounces it more clearly now but with great effort. Speech develops with greater ease and speed as the Creature acquires the use of more words. He begins to discourse, in an extremely long speech, borrowed from Mary Shelley's book, mainly from Chapter XI and also substantially from Chapters XIII and XIV. This is the Creature's famous account to Frankenstein of how it discovered light, darkness, fear, fire, the moon, a village of humans, the wickedness they are capable of, the stupidity of governments, laws, social classes, property, and at last hatred as the only remedy for the suffering of having been excluded. The Creature's account stops at the point where he is about to kill little William; in the novel it continues, to the pathetic conclusion, a request for a companion in its image. This is the Creature's account from the play:

"It is with a considerable difficulty that I remember the original era of my being: all the events of that period appear confused and indistinct. I saw, felt, heard, and smelt, at the same time. By degrees, I remember, a stronger light pressed upon my nerves, so that I was obliged to shut my eyes. Darkness then came over me, and troubled me; but hardly had I felt this, when, by opening my eyes, the light poured in upon me again. I walked. Before, dark and opaque bodies had surrounded me, impervious to my touch or sight; but I now found that I could wander on at liberty, with no obstacles which I could not either surmount or avoid. The light became more and more oppressive to me; and, the heat wearying me as I walked, I sought a place where I could receive shade. It was dark when I awoke; I felt cold also and half-frightened. I was a poor, helpless, miserable wretch; I knew, and could distinguish, nothing; but feeling pain invade me on all sides, I sat down and wept. Soon a gentle light stole over the heavens and gave me a sensation of pleasure. I started up, and beheld a radiant form rise from among the trees. I gazed with a kind of wonder. I felt light, and hunger, and thirst, and darkness; innumerable sounds rang in my ears, and on all sides various scents saluted me: the only object that I could distinguish was the bright moon, and I fixed my eyes on that with pleasure. I found a fire which had been left by some wandering beggars and was overcome with delight at the warmth I experienced from it. In my joy I thrust my hand into the live embers, but quickly drew it out again with a cry of pain. How strange, I thought, that the same cause should produce such opposite effects! I arrived at a village. How miraculous did this appear! The huts, the cottages, and houses engaged my admiration. The vegetables in the gardens, the milk and cheese that I saw placed at the windows allured my appetite. I entered one of the cottages; but I hardly placed my foot within the door before the children shrieked, the whole village was roused; some fled, some attacked me, until, grievously bruised by stones and many other kinds of missile weapons, I escaped. I obtained a knowledge of the manners, governments, and religions of the different nations of the earth. Was man, at once so powerful, so virtuous and magnificent, yet so vicious and base? To be a great and virtuous man appeared the highest honor that can befall a sensitive being; to be base and vicious appeared the lowest degradation. I could not conceive how one man could go forth to murder his fellow, or even why there were laws and governments; but when I heard details of vice and bloodshed, my wonder ceased, and I turned away with disgust and loathing. The strange system of human society was explained to me. I heard of the division of property, of immense wealth and squalid poverty; of rank, descent, and noble blood. And what was I? Of my creation and creator I was absolutely ignorant; but I knew that I possessed no money, no friends, no kind of property. I was, besides, endued with a figure hideously deformed and loathsome. Was I then a monster, a blot upon the earth, from which all men fled, and whom all men disowned? I learned that there was but one means to overcome the sensation of pain, and that was death. . . .

Each action, each sensation is accompanied by its representation by the occupants of the structure. The fire, for example, is pantomimed in the following fashion: Two actors lie on their backs, ass against ass, and "pedal" with their raised legs in the air, depicting flames. Another actor bends down, reaches out with his hand, and recoils when it gets "burned." The wickedness of men provoked by society is represented by scenes of violence between actors and in physical deformities—the latter to be used again in *Antigone*.

At the end of the account Frankenstein and his assistants notice that the Creature has disappeared, and set out to search for it in the auditorium.

Three flashes light up the Four Horsemen of the Apocalypse.

A policeman seizes the Creature on the stage and it strangles him. This generates a new act of "victimization." Actors spill into the auditorium, and afterward new acts of violence are committed in the structure. Directed by the Creature, teams of policemen set out to pursue the fugitives in the auditorium.

Darkness. In B3, the exact center of the structure, the only illuminated spot in the theatre, Death is seen riding an imaginary mount, facing the audience. Curtain.

Notes to Act II: In its final version, the second act lasts about one hour. In Venice, it had neither the legend of Icarus nor the legend of Buddha. Bella and Fritz were by Frankenstein's side. Elisabeth, the orphan who is betrothed to Victor Frankenstein in the novel, was also present, and confronted the Creature in disgust. The ego was then expelled through the mouth of the head. The monologue followed, and the Creature killed Fritz. The Four Horsemen and the act of repression at the end were added after Venice. In Venice, the functions of the mind turned into deformed monsters and went out in the world in innocuous guises. The faculties of the mind were denoted by Latin words (*videre, spirare, voluptas, creas, redemptio, mors*, etc.).

In Cassis, the play was performed under a full moon, a few yards from the sea. . . .

Comments on Act II: At the beginning of the act, everything is still possible. There is a feeling of spring, of innocence, of dawn. The Creature is delighted when it discovers colors and lights (the luminous poems); it opens up gradually to the magic of the external world, everything is marvelous as in a fairy tale; the Creature is like a child. But its awakening is a cruel one; the tempest of the spirit (the dream, the ship) is a trifle in comparison to the implacable harshness of human beings. They condemn and chastise a creature in the name of society because it is outside the acceptable norm, even though it has hurt no one. The Creature's intentions may be pure, but its appearance is repulsive; mistreatment gives birth to the spirit of revenge, which manifests itself in murder, the forbidden act. One passes from an April countryside to the cold and the desolation of winter. Innocence turns into crime and repression by the police, harmony among the faculties of the mind into cacophony and strife, transforming the faculties into victims and executioners. The many attempts at betterment—science, intellect, morality, levitation, Paracelsus, Freud, Wiener, Daedalus, Icarus, Buddha—all these have failed.[1] Icarus could not fly, Frankenstein has run aground. The audience is invited back to make the play "succeed"; one will have to see whether Frankenstein is able to resume the burden, whether some hope is to be retained at the end.

[1] To kill, to wish to fly, to create an artificial man, these are means for seeking illusory solutions. Prometheus (Frankenstein is for Mary Shelley "the Modern Prometheus") is punished because he brought fire to men.

26

FRANKENSTEIN, ACT III: What If They Succeed?

The Prison: Working in pairs, the executioners look for their victims in the auditorium. Once captured, the fugitives state their real identity (as actors) and answer all questions with a passive "Yes." They are taken back to the stage.

In A1, there is a clock, a roll of paper, ink, black shirts, and sheets of cardboard. They take the prisoners' fingerprints, give each a shirt, photograph them with a flash; then, upon a whistle signal given by the officer in charge, they move them on into A2 and dispatch them into the other compartments until all are filled. Each prisoner then draws a "curtain" of bars over the front of his cell. While the prisoners are passing from one compartment to another the lights go out, and the structure is silhouetted against the background, which alone is lit (in blue). Then the lights go on again, and each prisoner is improvising crazy screams and gestures; their faces are becoming masks; speech, a link, is banned: "World Action," a representation of the world. The whistle blows, the lights go out, the prisoners freeze; it blows again, they move on to the next cell. When all cells are occupied, the prisoners climb down again, then climb up again, producing the effect of a structure as permanent as the "brig," where the departure of a prisoner is annulled by the arrival of another. Here, no one is freed; there is only perpetual movement inside a machine that slowly, implacably, creates death.

Frankenstein is one of the last to be captured. He protests a little, and during the formalities he filches some paper; soon he will be giving the orders.

Fomenting the Revolt: The prisoners pick up

boxes lying in the corner of each cell, arrange them in the center of each level, and sit down on them with their backs to the audience. They are eating a meal together. The guards stand up; they are dressed like the prisoners, except that they wear caps. Two prisoners succeed in hiding a knife and a rope in their clothing.

All the prisoners are in bed. A guard is killed; then others, with knife and rope. To distract the guards who have not yet been overwhelmed, Frankenstein starts a fire in B5. It spreads. Glimmering red and smoke everywhere. Cries of dying prisoners. Silence.

The Countdown: Once the ringing of the alarm dies down, a mournful rattle rises. "Haaaaa. . . ." The "dead" drag themselves toward the center on all three levels. Little by little, they re-form the silhouette of the Creature, arms dangling, as at the end of Act I. The right hand holds a net, the left a lamp: weapons of "victimization." Will it start all over again? The countdown begins, and this time it is the Creature who is counting. Thirty seconds . . . twenty-five . . . twenty . . . zero. At zero, the Creature lights the lamp and shines it on the audience, then suddenly lets the net and then the lamp drop. The rattle turns into strong breathing, alive and steady. Slowly the Creature raises both arms in a gesture of greeting and peace. Curtain.

Notes to Act III: The last act is from thirty to forty-five minutes long. It has been changed more radically than the other two, not only structurally but also in spirit. In Venice, the fifteen compartments were so many miniature stages, as it were. A brief scene with dialogue was enacted in each one. Each scene had been based on a different Ibsen play, and the Creature moved from one compartment to the next, serving his apprenticeship in the world and in human relations, such as they are. In Solness, who had built a house in which men would be happy at last, the Creature recognized its creator. A desperate struggle took place, then Ibsen's characters seized the two enemies and ensnared them in two nets. The Creature, in another passage taken from Mary Shelley, bitterly reproached Frankenstein, who admitted having killed innocent people without having been able to stop the onslaught of events, once he was entangled in the mesh. At this, enmity vanishes, Frankenstein and the Creature embrace through their nets, the revolution of love triumphs, and everyone joins together to chant the closing lines from Aeschylus' *Eumenides*: ". . . no more violent untimely deaths to make the people few . . . no more sad scenes of violence, and wars, and early deaths . . . until happiness succeeds man's ancient need for hate." The Erinyes become the Eumenides. The characters prepare to make love (men + women, men + men, women + women, trios) and the loudspeaker announces that the law does not permit going any further.

The company thought that this ending was too optimistic, and the element of a happy ending displeased them. Moreover, they felt the use of Ibsen was rather obscure and the dialogue too sustained.

Comments on Act III: By virtue of its economy, simplicity, and sorrow, the last version is more in harmony with the preceding acts than the earlier one had been. The prison and the mad demeanor of the prisoners constitute a more expressive representation of the world than extracts from Ibsen could provide. The prison is the essence of *The Brig*; both stand for the world man has built for himself. The restrictions and the oppression in this act are not only external in origin; the three levels and everything that takes place on them are also the inversion of Act II—solitary compartments of the Creature's mind, modern man's mind. The structure becomes fully occupied, but the lines of communication are cut; everyone lives isolated from everyone else, and

Check thru Tape for cutting errors etc.

Tuning Anderson, Mary + Jenny : Check Maids cos, & proper
Control Booth Chic's costume

Light Man — Mon. 8:00 A.M.

Berlin
Sept 66

According to Julian, he was not thinking about anything specific when he made this drawing, but one could take it to be a view of the intertwined bodies of Frankenstein and the Creature.

madness takes root. The superman (the Creature) becomes the subman. Frankenstein protests being imprisoned in a punitive structure that he did not intend to create; nevertheless, the structure is the very result of his best intentions—his work has produced the antithesis of what he had hoped to create, and he himself is a victim of his own creation.

Frankenstein revolts, and the prisoners join with him. He wants to extricate himself, but once again he resorts to violence: he kills and causes others to kill. He has destroyed an evil social structure, but the final outcome is death. The fact that this death is brought about by means of fire is not a chance. In the novel, the Creature departs to light its own pyre; here Frankenstein does not set the fire to put an end to everything, but it gets out of his control.

If the prison is filled, it is because the arrested suspects refused to protest arrest. When they replied with the passive "Yes" they made themselves the executioners' accomplices. They acknowledged their guilt. Their "Yes" was negative, whereas their "No" in Act I had been positive. Here, they do not believe in the possibility of changing the world "here and now." Everything has turned against him. The prison, a large soulless machine, functions only because its gears—the prisoners—are well oiled.

This is a sign of inspiration for the Living Theatre. One sees it on the sweaters of pacifists, representing the initials of Universal Disarmament in visual Morse code. It also represents the tree of life and man raising his arms in a gesture of welcome, of peace, of joy, of love. . . .

The end, a sort of resurrection, much like the one Frankenstein attempted in Act I, but spontaneous, results in a new monster. Still, the cycle need not be endless; at "zero," the spectator is delivered to himself. However, the image which the spectator takes away is not the despairing one of a monster who holds the lamp and snare, symbols of the oppressive instruments of society, but one of a successful levitation . . . Return to zero. . . . He has discarded his instruments of torture and opened his arms. He is defenseless. He has love to give. He has set out toward a human "paradise," one made by man for man.

27

A SCANDALOUS EVENING

After Frankenstein *you didn't present a new production until* Antigone *in January, 1967. Meanwhile, on May 30, 1966, you offered an evening of "Free Theatre" in Milan which was to become the subject of a great deal of talk....*

JUDITH: *Sipario,* an Italian magazine devoted to the theatre, was celebrating its twentieth anniversary, and we were invited by the organizers of the affair. We suggested an evening of "Free Theatre," and they were very enthusiastic about it. First we were thinking of doing part of *Mysteries,* even though I was extremely reluctant about the whole thing because of the party atmosphere. Anyway, the organizers were duly informed, and the spectators were given a mimeographed notice saying, "Free Theatre. This is free theatre. Free theatre is invented by the actors as they play it. Free theatre has never been rehearsed. We have tried free theatre. Sometimes it fails. Nothing is ever the same.—The Living Theatre." The evening was very lively. In contrast to what we had done at the premiere of *Mysteries,* we didn't decide on a theme; the only thing we decided was not to speak at all and leave when one hour had passed. Without any previous discussion, we formed a compact group in the middle of the crowd. We were very serious, we didn't even stir; our silence was in effect a deep feeling of belonging to our community, a meditation. We were existing, intensely. It was not a trance, mind you, because we remained thoroughly aware of being a community. The people there poked at us, embraced us, tried to make us react. After experiencing their movements and our silence for three quarters of an hour, we left.

Afterward, we faced a tremendous problem. People said—and some are still saying it—that we didn't "perform." Whether it was theatrically interesting, dramatic, successful, these are not criteria. The only criterion is that we did perform, as far as the concept of "free theatre" went. Still, even very perceptive friends of ours, like Cathy Berberian who was there that night and performed with us, thought that we didn't perform. Well, we did, and so we compelled people to ask themselves a fundamental question: What is a theatrical event?

JULIAN: Exactly. We gave the only possible answer to that particular party situation. It was one of the most successful choices in my life. The confrontation was really *troublesome* to the guests. They wanted to be led in an entirely different direction; they didn't want to be where they were, yet they *could not* extricate themselves. They reacted like people who go to a happening and expect the provocation they have paid for. It was a reaction of *anger*, and it was expressed in a material form as well, inasmuch as the money collected for the Living Theatre during the evening was never turned over to us.

You didn't get paid?

JULIAN: Yes, we were paid in advance. I am referring to the voluntary contributions of the guests. The tension was so great that the police were called in and the evening became one of the twelve scandals of the week in Italy. There are twelve scandals a week in Italy. . . .

JUDITH: The provocation that was not intended to be so may well have taken place. In the final analysis, it was a very deep one. The negative aspects of the evening—all that harsh controversy—were really the positive aspects. The effect we produced was infinitely stronger than if we had shouted or spoken. People would have been satisfied, but they would certainly have believed that the whole thing was a failure. In our judgment, we did perform because we transformed a specific atmosphere into an entirely different one. Then we left, because there was nothing more that could have emerged.

On March 27, 1967, you gave a single performance under the title "World Action," in Perugia, Italy.

JULIAN: That was closely related to *Frankenstein*. We presented part of the third act to a student organization in a typical Italian theatre, except that we seated the audience in the pit and performed using the boxes as prison cells, which is what they are. By virtue of this set-up, the actors achieved an exceptional degree of automatism, in the sense Breton employs the term. The performance lasted for half an hour.

To complete the dossier of your special presentations, there was one in Bordeaux on November 17, 1968.

JULIAN: First, Silvano Bussotti, dressed as Harlequin, presented a satire on critical pieces written about his *The Passion According to Sade*. After a fifteen-minute intermission, we followed with *All'-Italia*,[1] a composition by Bussotti for twenty-four players, based on a verse by Pasolini: *"sprofonda in questo tuo bel mare, libérà il mondo."* With the composer's permission we conceived an interpretation in the form of solos, followed by duets, and then by choir. We also used our bodies. Bussotti wanted as intuitive an interpretation as possible. The Pasolini verse was not sung; it was spoken in unison at the beginning, and then by a single voice during the recital and at the end.

---

[1] The Bussotti play received very unfavorable reactions from the audience. They were greatly offended and wreaked havoc in the auditorium. The Living Theatre was well-received.

28

ANTIGONE: From Sophocles to Brecht, From Brecht to the Living Theatre

Judith and Julian took a side trip to Athens during the first European tour in 1961. While there, they bought the *Modellbuch* of Brecht's *Antigone*, which was published shortly after the world premiere of the play in Kur, Switzerland, in 1948. It was a large album containing the text, Brecht's stage directions, and a great many photographs of the performance. The play struck them as a true celebration of civil disobedience.

Brecht based his play on Hölderlin's translation, which followed Sophocles step by step. Nevertheless, Hölderlin did make some subtle modifications that affect Antigone's relationship to the gods. When Kreon asks Antigone why she trespassed the law and covered the corpse of Polyneikes—and in the Greek world only the dead whose corpses have been burned or buried can lie in peace—she answers, in Hölderlin's version: "That's it: my Zeus did not forbid it to me. . . ." In Sophocles, she says: "It is not Zeus who made this restriction to me." His translation introduces ambiguities that deserve thorough examination but need not concern us here, because Brecht's attraction to Hölderlin was focused mainly on the value of his poetry. The relationship with the divinity has been eliminated in Brecht's adaptation, with the action unfolding on the human level and in political terms.

Let us see how the brothers become enemies. In the Greek version, Oedipus is succeeded on the throne by his incestuous sons, Eteocles and Polyneikes. They agree to divide the inheritance, ruling in alternate years. At the end of his first year of

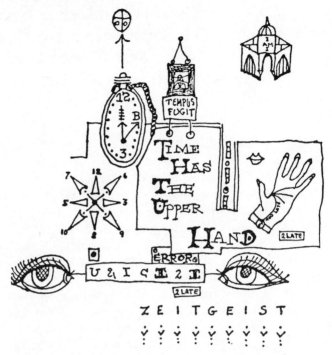

These variations on the theme of the passage of time by Judith Malina were improvised shortly before the premiere of *Frankenstein*.

kingship, Eteocles refuses to make way for Poly-neikes, who then enlists the aid of Argos in claiming his right. In the subsequent battle, the Argive army is routed and the brothers kill each other. Their uncle, Kreon, becomes king of Thebes. One of his first acts is to order a hero's burial for Eteocles, who died for Thebes, and forbid the burial of Poly-neikes. (A grievous injury, for the dead could not enter Hades without burial in the ground.) Antigone violates Kreon's edict in order to obey the overriding law of the gods, which commands her to accord the same right to Polyneikes as was accorded to Eteocles. Kreon, despite the warning of the seer Tiresias not to defy divine laws, condemns her to be entombed alive in a cave. Kreon's son, Haemon, who is Antigone's fiancé, kills himself at her feet, after she has hanged herself in the cave. Eurydice, Kreon's wife, also kills herself. Kreon is now alone, and the house of Labdakos (Oedipus' ancestor) will vanish with his death.

In Brecht's version, Eteocles is a "good soldier" who fights for Thebes, without concern for matters beyond that. Polyneikes is a deserter who refused to participate in a war that seemed unjust to him; he flees upon seeing Eteocles' body trampled upon by the warriors' horses. Kreon has been ruling for some time, and the war is being waged for the possession of the iron mines of Argos. It is an economic war: he who has iron, has arms. (In his prologue to the play, Brecht depicts another Antigone, another Ismene, in Berlin, 1945, finding their brother hanged from a butcher's hook in the street for having deserted the Nazi armies. In the author's mind the prologue could be replaced by something else: slide projection, etc.)

Brecht leaves Eurydice out of his version, but, unlike Sophocles,[1] he appends the story of Megaros, Kreon's second son, and makes him die in battle. Antigone is neither a heroine nor a revolutionary in Brecht's adaptation; what she does is just, but she does it too late. She ought to have opened her eyes sooner, as others ought to have opened theirs. She buries Polyneikes, because Kreon's law is human law, therefore it may be broken by humans. Brecht's *Antigone* is the tragedy of "too late!" The chorus is turned into the elders of Thebes by Brecht; they accept Kreon's deeds by their silence. Toward the end, when they can no longer ignore the catastrophe

---

[1] Sophocles says only that before her death Eurydice accuses Kreon of having caused the death of her two sons. The full story is to be found in Euripides' *The Phoenicians*: Megaros was to be killed to please the gods and bring victory to Thebes. But Kreon refused to kill him and Megaros committed suicide on the walls of Thebes.

Kreon has brought upon them, they abandon him. But it is too late by then, for the catastrophe is their own extermination.

The essential element in Brecht's version is the transposition of the divine aspect into a political one. This does not mean, however, that all irrational residues have been filtered out. The gods may have vanished, but Antigone's consecrated devotion has been preserved, along with the very obscure myths related by the chorus, the mystery of which was liked by Brecht, who seems to have made up some myths of his own, like "the brothers of Lachmyia" (verse 547), which are totally unknown in Greek or world mythology.

Judith Malina's English translation is very precise. It is rendered in free verse, wholly faithful to Brecht's text. Where Brecht clings to Hölderlin, she follows word by word; where he veers off, she strives to retain the meter of Brecht's German in the translation. She began working on the text in 1961, and completely reworked and revised it several times before she regarded it as suitable to be placed in rehearsal. Except for very minor cuts, the play was performed in its entirety, although the prologue was replaced by a pantomime and accompanying sounds.

During Brecht's rehearsals for the premiere of the play in Kur, the actors who were put at his disposal, except for the great Helene Weigel, had only the slightest experience with the technique of "distancing" (*Verfremdungseffekt*) that Brecht invented. Accordingly, he devised a sort of connective text for the rehearsals; an actor announced what was happening and thereby was prevented from counting on the element of surprise in interpreting his role; the "distancing" defused the action in advance and emphasized the mythological, archaic, and historical aspects of the character. The Living Theatre distributed this text—which was turned into captions for the photographs in the 1954 edition of the *Modellbuch*—among a number of actors who recited it in the language of the audience, in the clearest and most didactic manner they could achieve.

Wherever the company may be performing, the stage always represents Thebes, and the auditorium (and occasionally the apron) Argos. When the action moves to the auditorium, the house lights go on. The lighting is intense and unvarying throughout the play.

The stage is bare, without sets or curtain. Every actor—there are more than twenty—is always on stage, whether the stage or the auditorium is the place of action. The actors wear everyday clothes, but no gaudy jewelry—mostly undershirts, blue jeans, gym shoes, or no shoes at all. Judith wore a sleeveless black shirt and black slacks as Antigone; it was the costume best suited to conceal her pregnancy at the time of the opening. She kept the same costume afterward.

There were no props at all. When a seat for Tiresias was called for, an actor would lie down on his back, raise his backside, and provide a prop for the seer. Kreon, opposite, rests on a throne formed by the Elders. When a battering ram had to be raised against Argos, two actors would lift a third with flexed muscles above their heads, and move him in the manner of a steam hammer. Antigone walks on the back of a crouched actor—a slave—it is said that she, too, "has eaten bread baked in humble ovens," thereby acquiescing in the iniquity of Thebes' social structure.

The sound effects are constant and varied, produced entirely by the actors' voices and bodies. An actor punctuates the rhythm of a dance of Bacchus for three quarters of an hour by clacking his tongue and slapping his palm against his thigh. At times, the sounds are imitative: wind, waves, the subdued breaths of sleep; at times analogical: Hindu or Gregorian chants. One might say, with Judith, that the production is "staged with total sound."

Many events in *Antigone* are not enacted but

merely reported in the Brecht version: battles, the death of the brothers, the burial of Eteocles, the death of Polyneikes, Antigone's recovery of the body. There are also mythical events, such as the evocation by Antigone of the sources of her inspiration— their glorious deaths. All these are mimed by the actors, including the most obscure passages of the chorus; the actors turn themselves into pliable plastic. They descend into the auditorium three times. The first time, it is to mime the battle in which Eteocles and Polyneikes perish; then, following an intonation by an actor, to be the chorus and chant about the monstrosity of man, their arms raised in the manner of the Creature in *Frankenstein,* virtually embracing the audience;[2] finally, to emit a rambling, hollow sound from time to time, upon the death of Megaros, who had been in the audience throughout, as if to indicate that the events unfolding on the stage are but the visible surface of a deeper, permanent struggle in Thebes. The actors never leave the stage during the play except to go to the auditorium.

The verses Brecht assigns to the Elders have been divided between them and the People. (The Elders are made into Kreon's docile instruments. He has castrated them on stage.) Among the inhabitants of a city, there are certain citizens clever enough to become senators, without ceasing to remain members of the citizenry, in order to sustain a tyrant. Tyrants exist only by the complicity of the people, or their elected representatives, and by citizens who choose to abrogate their rights at a

[2] The verses attributed to the Elders are divided between the Elders and the People. Sometimes the Living Theatre gives one verse to one single person: Polyneikes, the "agent" of all that happens, stops the dance of Bacchus. Sometimes also all the actors speak the lines. Kreon and the other main characters existing no more as such. During the chant on man's monstrosity, Antigone and the guard are alone on a stage, while the audience is enveloped in the poetry of the marvels and horrors man can accomplish.

given moment. Kreon prevails only by virtue of being propped up in this manner; he is but a gear, turning only because other gears are turning. This is why he is so often placed in the center of a diffuse group of Thebans when he speaks his lines; he is a creature of many heads, a many-limbed dragon, a brittle creature who falls down more than once in the course of the play.

It would be too simple to point a finger at the guilty. The evasion of responsibility, the dissolution of a character, of an individual among the masses, is a complicity. This is also why the Bacchic celebrations of the Thebans are not interpreted as simple *joie de vivre* but—more significantly—as something communicated, controlled from a distance by Kreon, the way he controlled the soldiers' movements at the beginning of the play, making them into the arms and legs of a Kreon (in the manner of Frankenstein's Creature) by a masturbatory caress. The people are "absent." The events in Thebes and Antigone's disobedience alarm him, but he chooses not to think further about them.

The Living Theatre declines to accuse the "most guilty"—Kreon, in this case—or to spread the guilt so as to cover everyone equally; instead, it suggests various degrees of guilt. No one is blameless; if Thebes is the way it is, the fault lies neither entirely with Kreon—because then the spectator would identify with the innocents, that is, everyone else—nor entirely with the Thebans. A Kreon must exist in order to profit from the situation; it is easy to become a Kreon.

To talk about collective responsibility is to be inexact. The Living Theatre dramatizes very precisely the responsibility of each individual, which is a different matter altogether.

This concept is worked out at the actor-spectator level in the following manner:

Prologue: While the audience is filling in and settling down, the actors come on one by one, facing the spectators. They form groups, then re-form other groups. The stage and the auditorium are lit up. The actors' expressions are set and hard, seldom individual. Actor looks at Spectator without any amenities. Thebans looking at Argives. The spectators are ill at ease. They have come for a "feast," and they are being regarded with severity. They have been dethroned. There is hostility in the air, or at least there is no frivolity. The actors are even prattling at times, showing no respect for the spectators who have paid to see them as in *Mysteries* and *Frankenstein*. When the atmosphere of hostility is clearly established, the actors, who heretofore have been merely assessing the enemy, pass to a state of war. They crouch, cover their heads with their arms, and intone a siren-like wail. A few moments later, Kreon sends his warriors to Argos. When the battle is over, a long silence follows, then the first lines of the Antigone legend are spoken by Judith, and the scene between her and Ismene takes place. At the end of the play, when Thebes is helpless, the troupe repeats the device of the opening scene. Now Thebes is defeated by Argos—that is, by the audience—and the Argives are preparing the extermination. Assembled in a row at the edge of the stage, the actors await the closing line of the chorus; then, while the audience begins to applaud, the actors become terrified of the fate reserved for the Thebans and confront the spectators, who are about to leave a nightmare to think about "art." The troupe compels them to face reality yet once more by expressing a dreadful terror as they retreat, trembling, to the back of the stage, where they huddle in fright, as if pursued by assassins or as if fleeing deadly gas. "What have we done?" Darkness.

Kreon and Antigone: Kreon is not interpreted as a stiff monarch, but as a military commander who ambiguously alternates flattery, violence, and foolish drivel—the latter passing for wisdom in the eyes of the people who do not perceive that

and the groans won from the stricken ~~coast~~ (place)

Haimon is coming.

on her dread bridle bed.

Son There's a rumor you've come.

You've slain many people—

Line by line sketches by Judith Malina choreographing movement for a scene in *Antigone.*

this sort of "good fellow" behavior is the most effective type of cleverness. The people are completely preoccupied with their little concerns, as said; they are far less conscious than Kreon. The set purpose of the action requires that a "mental deformity"—the people's all-absorbing concern for personal well-being, in this case—find a physical form in the performance. This is in evidence with the

Thebans, and at times with Kreon. But never with Antigone, for her thoughts dwell only on sacred matters.[3] The examples of ancient heroes have taught her to exalt in having a holy death like Danae. She lets herself be intoxicated by this arrogant pride, but soon seizes hold of herself—a determined little girl who does not want to be indebted for her own death to anyone or anything, except herself. She is anarchistic and she encourages anarchy; her fault is that she is too late. What she does is exemplary but belated; besides, the example is not followed, and this is what is so dreadful at the end. The Thebans no longer have a way out: there had been time, there is no time any more. In the concise formulation of André Bonnard,[4] "The existence of Antigones is what constitutes the promise and exigency of a new society, remade by the measure of man's freedom."

Imagery: The only way to do justice to the wealth of imagery would be to film the performance. A written account must be content to restrict itself to approximations, reinforced by a few examples.

The sources of inspiration were various. "We have tried to introduce as many images as possible, of as many origins as possible," Julian explained. Most importantly, painting and sculpture served as such origins. Brecht could have taken out the secondary myths and the discourses of the chorus, but he did not. There is a substantial amount of mysticism in a number of passages. Accordingly, it was natural for the Living Theatre to draw on religiously oriented inspiration, especially in view of its commitment to unify spectator and actor. It was no less natural to turn to Greek imagery—vases, friezes—and also to

[3] Antigone is also the Anti-woman (anti-gune), the one who chooses the family, the brother, instead of love (Hæmon). She is the defender of a very archaic society. Judith is very conscious of that in her acting.

[4] André Bonnard, *La civilisation grecque*, Vol. 2. La guilde du Livre, 1954, p. 34.

Egyptian bas-reliefs. (Standing on the apron of the stage, Antigone assumes the pose of an Egyptian pharaoh, her arms crossed in front of her, while on each side of her four Elders reproduce in profile the silhouettes of Egyptian priests who bury the dead.)

The imagery is never redundant; it always enriches the scene. When a triumphal arch is called for, to mark the so-called triumph of Thebes, a phantom column is contrived in the back of the stage, to indicate the illusory character of the triumph. It is a sort of pathetic funeral monument, the idea coming from tombstones as well as from the three-level totem poles of the North American Indians. First, the idea of a composition imitating a Roman column was considered, but the phantom column was more interesting to the troupe, because in addition to an immediately compelling plasticity, it was charged with meaning. The column was composed of three dead bodies; thus not only the "triumphs" but their commemoration as well were built on the dead. Here, the significance of the composition was strengthened by the idea that the bodies were not simply slain soldiers but those of the three who had given their lives for the sake of protesting war and Kreon's unjust law: those of Polyneikes, Antigone, and Haemon.

A number of images evidently created a certain ambiguity in the play that could be subjected to endless analysis; they are ambiguous by virtue of the abundance of meaning contained within them. When Ismene begs her sister to let her partake in her duty, Antigone is encircled by four actors forming a cell. As Ismene speaks, they cover their ears, thereby denoting all at once the cell, the thick walls, and the "fortress of resolution" Antigone is erecting, for she is frail and needs courage.

Antigone's actions when she is gathering the dust for burying Polyneikes is another example of abundance. At first, a jug resembling the jug used by

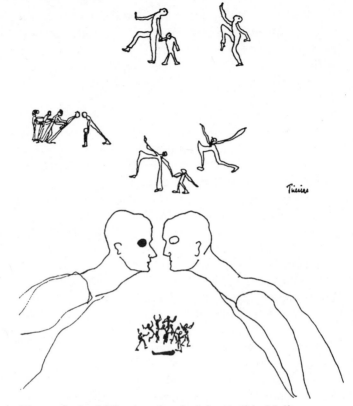

The arrival of Tiresias sketched by Judith Malina.

Helene Weigel at Brecht's premiere was considered. In the end Antigone's body became the receptacle; she deposits the dust she gathers on her knees in her mouth. Each gesture of depositing is accompanied by a mournful intake of breath ("haaa. . . ."), because the body makes contact with dead matter, followed by an eased exhalation ("heee. . . ."), because the life of the body communicates itself to the dead matter. Antigone's gesture is a representation of Polyneikes' resurrection in the form of a revolutionary impulse: She gives "life" to Polyneikes by rebelling, as she gives "life" to the dust she deposits in her mouth. This abundance of meaning, this interpretation at multiple levels of little rationality would not have been coherent if the Living Theatre had not moved forward step by step. The chorus passages—and Brecht himself was aware of their obscureness—were endowed with a patiently evolved character of plasticity, and were molded and remolded constantly. Brecht also retained certain obscure sections from Sophocles to which the troupe gave a clean interpretation, such as the guard's terrified report that Polyneikes' body had been buried, although no footprints, wheelmarks, or signs of tools could be found, that it had been done by someone neither human nor animal. Who could have committed the act? The Living Theatre found the solution in a phantom—Antigone's phantom, her "double." During his report, the guard raises Antigone by the waist, she places her feet upon his, and in this position he walks her to Polyneikes' body. Her eyes are widened, her mouth forms an O. She enacts a series of mysterious gestures over the body, thereby illustrating the guard's secret thought: A phantom has done it. Then she exclaims, "Stop that," aimed at Kreon, who does not like nonsense, and runs off emitting the sound—"rrrrr. . . ."—of a little girl committing a prank. As she runs off she touches the trembling Thebans as a child would touch the poles of a fence, rattling them as she scoots by. The spell is broken.

Polyneikes' Body: The entire play pivots around Polyneikes' body. For two hours the actor playing that role lies rigidly on the stage. He is concentrating intensely. At times on the apron, at times in the back of the stage, he is always in the sight of the spectators. He is the "magnetic pole" of the play, according to Judith, although he is never seen in Brecht's version. The body is the evidence of Kreon's errors and injustice, the body is the cause of Antigone's and Haemon's revolt. It symbolizes a death that weighs heavily in the balance of the destiny of Thebes. It symbolizes the past, the errors of history, an injustice that could have been averted, but having been done it exercises an influence on the present. One cannot kill and forget. When Ismene is demanding a part in the sacrifice at the beginning of the play, Antigone turns her sister's head toward the corpse. Then she places it in Ismene's arms, and Ismene collapses under the weight, the body obliterating her own. The obsessing presence of the body constitutes a warning. This warning becomes even clearer when the Elders address Kreon while placing on his head the mask of Bacchus (represented by a wide, lifeless smile): "May he who has troubled you, mighty one, praise you. Don't drive him down so deep that he lies out of sight, for in that direction he lies, on the ground, naked, to confront you. He is resigned to his shame; hideous and horrified, abandoned to his loss, dehumanized, he remembers his earlier form and rises and is new."[5] Carried by Haemon and Antigone, Polyneikes is held high and marched triumphantly above Kreon's fallen body, signifying the end of the tyrant, the glory attained by the act of revolt. Polyneikes "lives," because he said "No" to death, because his revolt generated the revolt of others. The Living Theatre is proclaiming the primacy of life, for between Kreon and Polyneikes the dead one is not the one who lost his life.

[5] See photo insert.

29 | "PERHAPS ONE DAY WE'LL BE A WHOLLY ANARCHIST COMMUNITY. ..."

The Living Theatre has been subjected to a lot of nasty criticism in regard to Antigone, *because you play Brecht in your own way. It has been said that the war with the audience was childish. ...*

JULIAN: Maybe it was childish. For us, the most important moment is the ending. If the ending is successful, the whole play is successful. If people feel how atrocious it is to kill each other, if they feel it physically, then perhaps they'll be able to put an end to it.

JUDITH: Antigone is a pacifist. Her struggle is for love, the same way a pacifist's is—facing the police, for example. At the same time, there is something childish about her. What is very strong about her is her ability to refuse to die the kind of "formal" death that the Elders suggest to her. She wants to be an "example."

Not using costumes once again was another invitation to be attacked, was it not?

JULIAN: We wore practical clothes, ordinary work clothes. If we had worn "polite," bourgeois costume, that is to say something that we did not or could not wear all the time, then we would have been saying that we the Living Theatre are apart from it; that we criticize from the height of a pedestal or from outside the society we depict. We feel as responsible for the state of things as does the public. We are not doing enough to effect a change for the better. However, it is necessary to realize that we cannot give people solutions in the theatre where we are engaged in searching for the salvation through theatre. It is simply not possible. It is only possible *with* the public. Perhaps by searching together we'll find it. What we are saying to the public is, We are with you, among you. . . . The act of performing, of becoming someone else—which is what always astonishes the spectator—has taught us some very valuable lessons. When the actor succeeds in performing, in understanding his role as the Guard, or, collectively, as the State, then he acquires a much clearer idea of the mechanisms that destroy man. In this we are not placing ourselves above the public; we are saying that they may serve their own apprenticeship in studying that mechanism, just as we do, and perhaps eventually cast it off. . . .

So far you have not developed an "anonymously" conceived production, as you have been wanting to. Judith Malina and Julian Beck always sign their names to all of them.

JULIAN: We are getting closer to it. I would say that *Frankenstein* was collectively created. The problem was that during the last five or six weeks before Venice it was no longer possible to have twenty-five directors on stage. The pieces of the puzzle had to be assembled. Judith and I were holed up in the hotel room. Then the same thing happened the following year, before Cassis and for *Paradise Now* in 1968. We put the pieces together. The actors were free to express themselves in the way they wanted to. During rehearsals, there were always some actors sitting in the auditorium, giving their opinions. For *Antigone,* we had months and months of discussion. We wanted to establish a distance from the *Modellbuch,* but we didn't know how to go about it. The success of *Antigone* has been very important. It seems to us that from now on we can perform anything, even Shakespeare. . . . We started back from zero for *Antigone* after the Cassis festival in 1966. The organizers were kind enough to let us stay on for three weeks afterward, but nothing came into focus. We were completely dried out. It wasn't till October that the chorus of the brothers of Lachmyia began to shape up in our minds. It was absolutely imperative that we find a means of conveying to the spectators that the abandonment of responsibilities in *Antigone* was their concern. Little by little, the play started to evolve around the first chorus.

Was it in any way helpful to you to have seen Grotowski's The Constant Prince *at the Théâtre des Nations?*

JUDITH: To see someone communicate with the body in such a directly personal way was obviously useful for us. We were astonished to find that although we were moving along parallel lines, the resemblance between us was very faint. We were equally surprised by his strict discipline, his method. Moreover, we sometimes obtained comparable results through an extremely personal lack of disciplinary methods. I think it is simply because we live in the same epoch.

JULIAN: I saw only a small part of the performance but I was struck by it immediately. I recognized immediately that it was in direct relationship with what we were sketching for our *Antigone* rehearsals. Besides, the manner of Grotowski's adaptation of Calderon was quite close to ours in respect to Mary Shelley. I was greatly encouraged, because I saw proof that what we wanted to do could work; it was working!

When did you begin the exercises for utilizing the voice in relation to different parts of the body?

JULIAN: With *Frankenstein*. The idea came to us from the voice itself! We noticed that certain sounds can be produced properly only when they are correlated with a specified body action. Accordingly, when a part of the body undertakes a movement, it "dictates" the proper sound. We have always worked toward harmonization. There is a wide open field for applying this principle. We live in a schizophrenic society where everything is partitioned off, beginning with the individual's internal solitude. It is essential to change that, to put the heart, the brain, and everything else into communication with each other. . . .

When you are directing, how do you divide the work?

JULIAN: The actors make all sorts of contributions. Judith understands them very well. She utilizes whatever technique may be best suited to each, because they come from different backgrounds.[1] She doesn't speak in terms of theory; she tells them just the right things to set their imaginations working and give them, I believe, a feeling of freedom. She inspires them. She senses what will make an actor arrive at useful discoveries. She doesn't tell them anything that will trouble them or add to the confusion, if there is confusion. With me, it's very different. I offer the actor poetry and theory. I propose improvements in visual arrangements: "The scene will be stronger if there's a group in this or that spot." Judith is always very practical; she'll find a reason why a group should be in a given place at a given time. She doesn't give orders. She'll ask the actor, "Don't you think that the character will now want to . . . ?" I was always struck by her knack for creating atmosphere.

Your actors have often been criticized for a certain amateurishness, more noticeable in some than in others. Obviously, one cannot ignore the fact that you travel—too much—and that the actors are first of all members of a community.

JULIAN: Our actors are young. Most of them, anyway. It seems to us that if they are not as accomplished as those who have spent years in drama schools, they are in turn quite free in regard to the very artificial atmosphere that reigns over the "theatre world." They are seeking a means of ex-

---

[1] Many had taken drama courses at college, several had worked in television, theatre, nightclubs, movies; one had made her debut on Broadway and in the movies as a child. A good many are experienced writers, painters, or musicians.

pressing themselves more deeply in the theatre. The work goes much faster with the type of actors we choose, because they are eager to change the world and change the theatre. Maybe sometimes they don't know too much, but all the same, these are young people who very sincerely want creative work, and not careers. . . . As to collective direction, that's still another matter. We believe that the actors could become much more creative than they are. But they must learn to speak, to communicate; for example, some of them have a habit of addressing other actors in a certain manner that's bound to evoke hostility. They must learn to change their tone. They must learn to eliminate all manifestations of authoritativeness.

Are you still far from the point where you would think that your goal has been achieved?

JULIAN: I believe that the community is in some way the most important aspect of our work. It's also perhaps the least well realized, the least well perfected at the moment. It's more a concept than reality. We'd like this community to function truly like an anarchist society. When we speak of free society, we mean that it is necessary to create a society where the group is not sacrificed to the individual any more than the individual is to the group. The ultimate goal of our theories is a society without authority. We will be free to cooperate, to work together. Obviously, to talk about these things on the stage and not practice them would be a mockery. It must be made real in one's own life. Judith and I make a real effort to disappear into the community, to blend into it. We wither away little by little, as we want the state to do. But there is a long road ahead yet. We already function as an anarchist group, wherever we can; we share equally in the money we take in. Some members concern themselves with contracts and money matters, and they make the decisions. Spiritually and psychologically, the community is already anarchist. We'd like to reach the point where the theatre work itself becomes a truly collective enterprise. Judith and I still occupy a central position, so one cannot say that the goal has been reached.

But do you think that all the actors have creative gifts?

JULIAN: That's somewhat like asking whether or not the audience is capable of recognizing authentic inspiration in a work as it is presented to them. I know from experience that there are people who love to be very busy, and there are others who prefer to be less busy. We have to find out about that; we also have to find out what the members of the community really need as individuals.

I attended a rehearsal that was rather . . . unproductive.

JULIAN: True. We were very tired, as we often are. But then, there are magnificent rehearsals where the actors really collaborate. I must say that there's a lot of bitterness in the company on the part of actors who believe that others aren't interested enough in creative work. The critical spirit is highly developed. The actors argue an awful lot. In friendship, or also in anger, whichever the case may be. Once again, everything is not as it ought to be.

Where did this process originate in the history of the Living Theatre?

JULIAN: Even before *The Brig,* Judith and I have had this idea for years and years. At first, the actors didn't participate. The first time we spoke to them about it, it must have been in 1959, they said that all they wanted to do was act and get paid every week, if possible. If it wasn't possible, well, they would see what happened next, but meanwhile we should continue to take care of direction and administration, and they would continue to practice their profession. . . . An anarchist community cannot exist unless its members have certain perceptions and a certain knowledge; besides, they have to succeed in expressing the creativity they possess. Judith and I make it a point not to dominate so much on decisions. For example, the actors are always telling us about what they want to do, but by common agreement the casting is left to the two of us for every play. We have, I believe, a very good community, but it is in the process of full development still. Some of the thirty or so actors who came with us from the States have gone back. In the spring of 1965, there were forty-five of us. Some months after that, we began to function as a community without salaries; no one was paid wages any longer but received a share. We are now about thirty—I never count—with several children in early infancy. It is very important that the community become what we want it to be. I know very well that it would be possible to assemble a better group than ours, for the social and psychological problems have not been altogether resolved by us. Nevertheless, when we are told that an anarchist society is not viable, at least we can answer knowledgeably. It's difficult, certainly. It is our first goal to succeed in this effort, because if we do, then our experience can be reproduced anywhere, and another community like ours can be created in some other part of the world. Many of them. . . .[2]

[2] The Living Theatre has no entrance examinations, no rules. The only criterion is the possibility of harmonious development as a member of the community. If all those wishing to join were admitted, the community would have a hundred or two hundred members. For financial reasons alone, this is not feasible.

The members of the company form a soundly welded community, in spite of differences that are sometimes quite distinct. Among them are vegetarians, pacifists, anarchists, and those who are not committed to any of these causes.

From time to time, a couple will break up, another will form, but such realignments fail to affect the equilibrium of the community; this is not at all the case in other comparable communities, with the possible exception of the kibbutz. If an actor needs solitude to the point that he does not want to talk to anybody for a while—as happens from time to time—his needs will be respected. The actors are much happier with the Living Theatre than they have been anywhere else, whether they are Americans who were with the company when it arrived from the United States in 1964, or Americans who have joined it in Europe, or Europeans (Germans, Dutch, Austrians, Italians). In the opinion of the more thoughtful among them, the company is the most advanced form of human grouping in existence at this particular time.

30

WHAT PARADISE?

In January, 1968, the Living Theatre left for Cefalu in Sicily, where the seasonally vacant quarters of the Villagio Magico, operated by the Club Méditerranée, had been lent to the troupe. During the three months there and the subsequent three months in the Vieux Lycée Mistral that had been made available to the company in Avignon, the now famous *Paradise Now* production came into being.

The Becks' notebooks, which offer an excellent means of gaining insight into the company's tireless energy as well as into the recurring anguish and discouragement that accompany any creative effort, contain the fascinating account of how *Paradise Now* evolved from idea to staging. It was conceived collectively by the company and edited to its ultimate form by Judith and Julian. The whole thing was an incredible trip.

The Becks first discussed the idea for the play in Switzerland, en route to Italy. They arrived at the notion that a map they conceived to show the way to Paradise must be conveyed to the audience in some manner. To be sure, they had no idea at the time of how to achieve that purpose; the objective of the play itself remained to be defined. In discussion after discussion, before the map was conceived, the company pursued the concept of paradise, trying at least to catch a glimpse of its frontiers. The quest was further complicated by the fact that no one could readily agree on the essential nature of Paradise. Some clung to the belief that it was an exclusively metaphysical reality. Both Judith and Julian, however, insisted on the necessity of political signifi-

cance in the play. The result was a union—which I
call magical—of these two inclinations.

Although we will analyze the production of
Paradise Now in as great detail as we did *Frankenstein*, we will still be far from an adequate description. A writer's tools—words, periods, commas,
blank spaces for silence—are simply incapable of
rendering the phenomenon of *Paradise Now*. To
know the furnace, one must dare the fire. The methods of literary expression, poorly enough suited to
traditional theatre, are not even sufficient to describe the actual action of *Paradise Now*, let alone
the total experience of the play.

It has long been believed that analysis of a
theatrical work could be limited to two aspects: that
of form and that of acting. Comment on its structure, staging, characters, conflicts, plot, and performance of its actors comprised all that could be
said about a play. The work was treated much like a
novel or a poem. Whatever the spectator experienced was outside the critic's province.

Even today's psychoanalytical and phenomeno-
logical approaches cannot uncover the meaning of a
theatrical experience conceived as a real event. The
vibrations that emanate from the stage to the audience are still considered beyond the reach of analysis.

The reactions evoked in the audience, however,
raise the only real questions for critical interpretation—even in so-called normal productions in which
the audience has no part in hindering or altering the
progress of the play or changing the order and
content of its script. From the point of view that
ignores the audience's experience, there is no difference between Beckett and Shakespeare. This view-
point becomes completely untenable where *Mysteries and Smaller Pieces* and *Paradise Now* are concerned; the first inviting direct contribution from the
audience, and the second requiring this contribution
as an essential part of its composition, as it may lead,

theoretically, to the total abandonment of the play's original scheme in favor of the itinerary proposed by the audience.

Mysteries and *Paradise Now* are structured so much like real events that they actually assume a lifelike complexity, impossible to penetrate by means of rational description or formulas for emotions. There are too many unknowns and subconscious motivations beneath the surface of the action that far surpass the observer's conscious grasp.

An actual event, by virtue of its very reality, can make a much deeper impression on the brain than a symbolical, theatrical event. A murder on stage does not have the impact of an accident in the street. In the latter instance, something real has happened, even if—and this is an important point— the sidewalk onlooker does not remember such details as which of the colliding cars came from the right. Something real also happens in *Mysteries* and *Paradise Now,* which pieces are everything but reassuring. The barrier separating stage from audience has disappeared to allow the spectator a truer balance.

This has proven too much for some people, however. The embarrassment or disgust that lurks in the comments of critics and spectators betrays a fear of the unknown and the irrational. Like alchemists, the Becks and their company refuse to confine themselves to the restricted arena to which society has condemned the activity of the human mind. In the Middle Ages they would have been burned at the stake for such rebellion. Their very knowledge of the power of words enables them to realize that the spoken word is by no means the sole medium of communication among men. "We try to reach the spectator through many devices, many means," Julian told an interviewer for *The Maroon,* a student newspaper at the University of Chicago, "some metaphysical, penetration through the skin, the use of disturbing symbology, the stirring up of some emotions that we might regard as negative such as irritation, annoyance, hysteria, repulsion, boredom." In addition, the Becks claim to have learned from experience that a network of chemical and energy bonds links all beings and infinitely multiplies the exchanges among them. Indeed, some metapsychical people—as distinguished from spiritualists and astrologers—seem to possess an extraordinary extrasensory intuition for which a biological explanation will be very likely soon forthcoming. If instruments capable of gauging these forces are ever invented, we shall no doubt make some strange discoveries.

Although the Living Theatre has no such instruments at their disposal, they are convinced that these forces exist, and try by experimental methods to make use of them. Their distrust of "rational" dramaturgy has resulted from this exploration. It is something of an oversight that while much has been written in criticism of the naïveté of the political slogans in *Mysteries* and *Paradise Now*, no thought has been devoted to the mechanisms of prayer and incantation contained in both pieces.

It is said that the Living Theatre actor merely plays himself on stage. Instead of saying, as a traditional actor: "I am the embodiment of Richard III," or as a Brechtian actor: "I am Mother Courage, but I'm also Helen Weigel playing Courage," the actor in the Living Theatre says: "I am Julian Beck and I play Julian Beck." Even presenting oneself as an individual, however, requires maintaining oneself continually in the process of becoming. To touch with your rays other beings, you must be a sun. What the Living Theatre wants to accomplish in *Paradise Now* is a realization in each spectator that a transformation of his whole being is both possible and urgent; that he may pass from an imperfect state to lesser and lesser imperfection.

The rituals of the Living Theatre, in particular the ones contained in *Mysteries* and *Paradise Now,* serve the opposite purpose of church rituals. While church ceremonies are the codified expressions of a faith known and shared by its congregation, the Living Theatre's rites honor a "faith" for the most part unknown and unshared by the audience at the outset—the faith of revolutionary non-violence. The communication passes not from within to without, but from the exterior to within the content.

Paradise Now departs from the image of men running toward death and endangering the entire human race that was raised in *The Brig, Mysteries, Frankenstein,* and *Antigone.* The Paradise here lies neither in the heavens nor between the Tigris and Euphrates. It is not just another of those dreams which poets are so fond of that are won only to be lost forever. Man must create this Paradise by reinventing life. Paradise is the state of being that men will achieve when they have made a habitable world on this planet.

It is thus up to men to decide whether they will do so, or write yet another bloody chapter of history. Man's potential abilities can outstrip the machine's, put an end to massacre, feed all the world's populations, abolish money, law, government, armies, and borders. Nevertheless, be he the robber or the robbed, oppressor or oppressed, each person is playing along by the rules of a game that consumes him, yet that is only perpetuated because he wants it to be. The wildest dreams of Da Vinci and other visionaries of the past have come true, but over the same span of time man has woven a gigantic spider web above his head in which he struggles without even realizing it. Man believes that he is born free, but all his life he receives in his unconscious corrupt images that will hinder him from attaining true happiness. And happiness is only possible, after all, in a world where everyone may have at least the means of physical subsistence (every six seconds someone dies of hunger), and can be assured that he will not die at the hand of another. (How many tens of millions must be added to the count—too often considered exceptional—of Jews executed by the Germans in order to arrive at a fair estimate of man's murderous talents in the past fifty years alone?)

The world today belongs to the cunning and to their puppets. If a sufficient number of people would simultaneously renounce money and all its uses, they would initiate a golden age that would have no need of gold.[1] Paradise would be reality; the archetypal Genesis legends that treat the Golden Age as past will hold no more interest for men—Christians no less than others—and will be torn to shreds and blown away in the wind. Man will realize that he may throw off the burdensome yoke if he so wishes, for it was placed there by his own hand in the first place. This yoke is not part of the definition of man. It was just an *accident*.

[1] The alchemist-Living Theatre relation is already apparent. There is another parallel: the manufacture of gold would spell the ruin of the economy and ruling hierarchy, threatening both the State and its supporting Church. The Becks propose the abolition of the gold monetary standard, regarding it as a barrier between man and goods. The "danger" anarchism carries is, as one can see, of the same nature.

31

THE MAP AND THE TERRITORY

Paradise Now—does any play have a more beautiful title? When the spectator enters he is handed a chart that illustrates the structure of the production—the "map" conceived by the company. It is to be read horizontally from left to right, then vertically; each horizontal "rung" is numbered, and consists of three states—a Rite, a Vision, and an Action—which represent the actual sequence of events on stage. Pertinent information relating to each rung is given on the margins of the chart. Schematically, the play begins at the foot of the chart and moves on upward. The "Action" segment of the eighth (last) rung is called the Street.

The end of the play is left open. Some critics wanted to take the play for the revolution and the paradise the play speaks of. It is not so. Even if the audience feels, when they truly enter the structure and add to its beauty by their actions, a physical and mental exaltation bordering on ecstasy, the play remains nevertheless a *didactic practicing of joy*.

The Living Theatre strives to communicate the very taste of revolution. All social orders are maintained by tacit and hypocritical agreement among their members, the relationship between performer and audience in traditional theatre being but one example among many. *Paradise Now* audiences, however, suddenly discover that they are no longer the "privileged class" to whom the play is "presented," but are needed by the actors for the very accomplishment of the play. It is not only the actors who become creators in *Paradise Now*, but, what is still more revolutionary, the spectators as well!

There is, of course, wide variance in the degree of acceptance or rejection of this kind of freedom—a freedom that many spectators had never dreamed of, believing as they did that the world stands still. Some were able to complete only one lap of the journey. Others became angry and left. Still others embarked on their own acts (burlesques, shocked speeches, etc.) intended to disrupt the show. And others, with the help of the actors, got through the second level and beyond.

"The purpose of the play," Judith and Julian declare, "is to lead to a state of being in which non-violent revolutionary action is possible." Esthetic openness, however, is far from their intention. In attempting to induce this Paradise-Now feeling, the Becks could have made the mistake of creating a glittering production, resplendent with heroism and beautiful symbols—two hours of celestial visions with an intermission. Sipping his cold drink, the spectator would only find himself back in a life as insipid as before, with two or three more images of idyllic, unattainable joy. Shunning such banality, *Paradise Now* concentrates on conveying the realization that Paradise must be won through revolution. Revolution takes time, and the condensed representation of it accordingly lasts four or five admittedly taxing hours without intermission. There are moments of great joy, overwhelming discouragement, attacks, ambushes, doubts. The moments where the audience is invited to go to the next rung are entirely open to suggestions. The company does not at this point shift its role from that of guide to that of leader, but tries to develop the audience's ideas to their full potential.

By virtue of the random selection of spectators, their trips differ considerably. The spectators have come for reasons of curiosity, interest, or merely because they were able to afford a ticket. Most are not entirely accustomed to the idea of shedding their self-images they have so carefully created for their friends and the rest of the world. As the evening progresses, affinities are revealed among them and groups begin to form. People who have never met talk to each other. The theatre becomes a forum, a political meeting, the crossroads of impassioned exchanges, a *cour des miracles.* As they did in *Frankenstein,* the actors in this miniature of the revolution to come do their best to exorcise possible violence, in order to demonstrate the manner in which the overthrow of the old system must proceed. It is imperative that it take place without violence, so that the murderous system under which we now live may not be merely reproduced in another form. What violence could not accomplish in the course of history, nonviolence can. The Living Theatre itself has been reproached for the "violence" in *Paradise Now.* Judith feels that their critics have missed an important distinction. "A lot of people feel that every time you say something passionate, you're violent. (. . .) I think there is a great difference between passion and violence. I think politeness is the bane of the world. (. . .) I think that the politeness that takes place in the parliaments of the world is the most deadly murderous action going today," she told the interviewer from *The Maroon.*

We return to the diagram. The purpose of the play is the unification of the physical and spiritual individual, according to the proposition that the human being whose body lives in complete harmony with his brain, and whose mental faculties are happily balanced, attains a state of physical, mental, and spiritual jubilation that eradicates all urge of destruction toward his fellow man. In such a state, his only ambition is permanently to increase this joy.

This concept bears close relation to two of the major currents of spiritualist thought, the Cabalist and the Tantric. Like the anarchistic theories and other ideas previously mentioned, these two currents were warmly embraced by the Becks. The philosophy of each is illustrated in the diagrams of the human bodies, both with the feet planted at the first rung and the head reaching to the last so as to span both time and space in the theatrical production.

According to the *Cabala*, man is a microcosm. God created him in His own image to act as His instrument and intermediary in the macrocosm. Adam Kadmon (the bearded figure on the left) is the image of man as God's instrument, before the Fall. The Becks, who do not subscribe to the notion of the Fall and of original sin, concentrate their interpretation on the central meaning of the myth: man as the agent of perpetual creative force.

The eleven Hebrew inscriptions on the figure are *sefirot*, or the attributes of God, who permitted the creation. Moving from bottom to top—and from left to right where there are two inscriptions on the same level—we find, at ankle level, the physical Kingdom (*Malkuth*) or principle of forms, harmony of the world, essence of all the other *sefirot*. At the calves Victory (*Netzah*) or the triumph of life over death; and Glory (*Hod*), the eternity of the Being. At the thighs (some versions place them at the arms), Mercy (*Hesed*), which is infinite as is Severity (*Geburah*). At the sexual organs, Foundation (*Yesod*), cornerstone of stability. At the breast, Beauty (*Tiphereth*), which is without limits. At the neck or shoulder, Intelligence (*Binah*) in all its divine compass, equilibrated by Wisdom (*Hokmah*). Above the head the Crown (*Kether*), the guiding providence and source of all the other attributes. The highest inscription on the drawing is the Infinite (*En-sof*) and it is often confused with the Crown. Different versions sometimes term the *sefirot* differently, using, for example, Love for Mercy, or Foundation for Procreation.

The most exalted *sefirot* are situated near the top. The body of Adam Kadmon, with the *sefirot* superimposed upon it, serves as a representation of all the parts of Creation: Eternity, Foundation, and

Procreation of the physical world; Mercy, Justice, and Beauty of the moral world; and finally the metaphysical attributes of God, which might be said to comprise the intellectual world—Intelligence, Wisdom, and the Crown that is the Divine Providence or Will that created everything, including the other nine *sefirot*.

While we cannot undertake a lengthy exposition of what this High Wisdom represents, we can note that the actors were particularly interested in Hassidism, a modern form of the *Cabala,* and in one of its most original contemporary advocates, Martin Buber. In reaction against ascetic piety, Hassidism offers the Jew redemption in and by way of the world. The world is to be made better, and even the less learned of the faithful participate in this accomplishment. "Who turns away from the world in order to turn toward God," Buber says, "does not turn toward God in reality, but toward his own idea of God." The lower world upholds the higher world. (This Western mystic maxim has a Hindu counterpart in the Visvasara Tantra: "What is here is elsewhere: what is not here is nowhere.")

The *Manifesto* of Baal-Chem-Tov, the first Hassidic document, dated around 1736, is a cry of warning against "pure" speculation and the domination of the rabbinical clerics over the masses of the faithful. It calls for individual expression of feeling from each Jew and encourages practical rather than speculative interpretation of the *Cabala.* Clearly, a popular movement in the best sense of the word, and of an anti-intellectual bent, its central belief is that by and through man himself one may approach the Absolute.

The essential trip is the voyage from the many to the one, says the diagram—but also from the one to the many; the journey to paradise is as political as it is spiritual; as collective as individual; as exterior as interior. The figure on the right illustrates the ascension of the Kundalini—the primary rite of

Tantrism—and also follows this motif. Like the *Cabala* figure, it represents man as a microcosm. The Kundalini is conceived of as a sleeping snake, coiled between the sex organs and the rectum (perineum), and symbolizes the true creative power of man, the analogue of absolute creative power (*sakti*). The object is to waken the snake and make it work its way to the top of the body, where it is reunited with the absolute. The lower body represents the realms of hell, while the upper part from the base of the spine to the brain is comprised of the seven worlds, each marked by a lotus or "energy node" (*chakra*) bearing varying numbers of petals.

The first four-petaled *chakra* is located at the root of the spine. This is the seat of the earth element. The second, with six petals, is located at the bile ducts and is the seat of the water element. The third, with ten petals, at the navel, marks the fire element. The fourth, with twelve petals, at the level of the heart, is the seat of the air element. The fifth, with sixteen petals, at the pharynx, marks the seat of the ether element. Internal qualities (knowledge, conscience) reside in the two-petaled sixth lotus on the level of the eyebrows. The seventh lotus has a thousand petals and is located on the level of the brain. This is the seat of *Siva*.

As the Kundalini passes from lotus to lotus, it absorbs the elements therein, and the person attains a state of joy and supreme knowledge. We should note in passing that a theoretical understanding of *Paradise Now*, such as we have tried briefly to impart here, is not in the least indispensable to the spectator. An exclusively intellectual perception of the play is quite the opposite of what the Becks hope is the spectator's actual experience.

Before launching into description of the center of the diagram, which charts the action proper, let us decode the chart's remaining sections. In the column just left of the *Cabala* figure is a series of six horizontal lines, some whole, some cut in half. These

hexagrams are the coded answers furnished by the
I Ching to questions about the play posed by a
member of the company, Steve Thompson. The
translations of the code appear in the next left
column. Each of the three "answers" in each rung
corresponds to one of the three sections on the same
rung in the center of the chart. Thus, on the first,
"Progress" is the *I Ching's* answer to "The Rite of
Guerilla Theatre"; "Inner Truth" corresponds to
"Vision of the Death and Resurrection of the American Indian"; and "The Marrying Maiden" to "New
York City: Eight Million People," and so forth
through all the rungs. While some of these *I Ching*
answers may seem rather obscure to those readers
who resort to explications of that book, others are
of luminous clarity and guide the actors in their
improvisations of the corresponding stages.

Moving to the right, we come to the column of
colors along the left side of the Tantric figure. These
are the colors of the solar spectrum, progressing
from shadows to brightness. White at the top should
not be thought of as the absence of color but as
piercing clarity. Black signifies both the absence of
clarity and the combination of all colors, which
reside there in a state of dormancy or germination.
There is a certain dynamism in black. (According to
Hindu belief, black is the color of the tendency
toward disintegration—*tamas*: Shiva; white that of
cohesion—*sattva*: Vishnu.)

The first rung—the present world—is opaque.
Men cry out in the darkness. Stage lighting is regu-
lated in accordance with the spectrum of colors.
There is no "black" light on Rung I, but the stage
and theatre are lit as for a meeting or intermission.
Only the stage is lit for the "vision"; then the house
lights go up again for "New York." On Rung II, blue
appears in the "Vision" of the North Pole. The color
generally appears only at the moment of "Vision."

In the column on the right of the Tantric
figures are terms borrowed from Martin Buber's *The*

Ten Rungs.[1] The company had originally conceived the diagram in ten rungs because of Buber's classifications and the symbolism of the number ten, which is, for occultists, the number of numbers, the symbol of the cosmos. The number five also plays a major role in *Paradise Now*: five totems, five members to a cell, the Pentagon. For the Pythagorians as well as the Hindus, this was the numeral of life because it is formed from two, the first female number, and three, the first male number. (One is sterile, as it cannot multiply itself.) But in the end the company left out Pride-Humility and Service and rearranged the others in ascendent order from the Good and Evil to God and Man. (Buber held that spiritual ascension could start from any of the ten rungs. "There is no rung of being on which we cannot find the holiness of God everywhere and at all times." From this point of view, "evil too is good. It is the lowest rung of perfect goodness.")

The last column on the right shows what evils should be attacked in the corresponding rungs, and the proper forces to be employed in each effort. On the first rung, as clearly indicated, culture must be subjected to regenerative treatment. Our perception must be altered under esthetic assault so that we can reject our present culture, which is hierarchical, cut off from life, and an integral part of the oppressive system.

We now come to the actual action on stage. We should bear in mind, however, that such description must necessarily seem austere and inanimate. The map is not the territory, to speak in terms of semantics; and the gigantic, joyous ritual of *Paradise Now* can only be reduced to meticulous description at the expense of the richness of its living substance.

[1] New York: Schocken Books, 1947. Buber's Rungs are: 1. God and Man; 2. Prayer; 3. Heaven and Earth; 4. Service; 5. Teaching; 6. The Way; 7. Love; 8. Good and Evil; 9. Pride and Humility—Holy Wisdom; 10. Redemption.

32

PARADISE NOW: The Revolution of Cultures

Of the three stages on each rung of the journey to paradise, Rite is the impetus, the starter, the active symbol. As Judith explained to an interviewer,[1] the Rite stage sets the actors going and puts them in a preparatory condition by including something pleasurable to do or say or act out. It elevates them into a "spirited state." The Vision scene that follows is an intermediate state between action and elation, the clarification of the subject matter. The Rites, which are primarily physical activity, may be thought of as "rites of passage." (Thus the concept of a privileged knowledge owned by an elite and the exclusion of the others is abandoned here: because they are "of passage," the Rites are accessible to everyone. In this sense, the play does not concern esoteric but rather exoteric experience, to the extent that we can distinguish these categories here.)

The Visions are of a more cerebral nature and consist of dream images resulting from the Rites. The Actions are introduced by a text and then improvised with the collaboration of the audience. Although the spectator is not generally invited to participate in Rites and Visions, he nevertheless experiences what his senses and subconscious registers; and, stimulated by the energy thus generated, may then release his own energy in Action.

Rung I

A. THE RITE OF GUERILLA THEATRE. While the audience is taking their seats, the actors file

[1] *The Chicago Seed,* Vol. III, No. 4, January, 1969.

silently into the theatre. Approaching people here and there, separately, they declare in tones ranging from anguished confidence to neutral objectivity, "I am not allowed to travel without a passport." Whatever the reaction, verbal or otherwise, the actor repeats the sentence without engaging in conversation. The little statement becomes more intense; the actor remains detached from the surrounding people. After about two minutes of this all the actors let out a great shout—releasing, in effect, the mute cry that has welled up within everyone during the foregoing action. (Sometimes a spectator, in touching demonstration of the need to communicate, tries to help the actor. The actor, however, refuses all dialogue, for he is bent on the task of depicting the present world, which is everything but a Paradise. To speak at this point would only deny the present frustration.) When silence is restored, the actors utter another sentence in the same manner: "I don't know how to stop the wars." There is another joint shout; then the statement becomes: "You can't live if you don't have money." The next sentence is: "I am not allowed to smoke marijuana." The last: "I am not allowed to take my clothes off." Here, instead of ending with another yell, the actor angrily undresses in the midst of the audience, taking off as much clothing as the law allows.

As he shouts each of these five sentences, the actor becomes increasingly overcome by exasperation and suffering. The cry triggers a moment of transcendence in which he is freed from all the constraints of his present surroundings. This moment of release, when all energy is focused on a particular point, is called a "flashout." (There is a flashout after each sentence in the first Rite, after the resurrection of the Indians, after the Rite of Prayer, after the Rite of Study, the Vision of Apokatastasis, the Rite of the Mysterious Voyage, during the Vision of the Integration of the Races, at the end of the Rite of Opposite Forces, during the Flight in Hanoi-Saigon, and at the end of the Rite of I and Thou.)

These five "flashes" in the first Rite are swift sketches of the world of prohibitions in which we live:

"I am not allowed to travel without a passport." I cannot move about freely on this planet, which, after all, belongs in its entirety to each one of us. I live in a world of fear. I am bound to that corner of the earth where pure chance delivered me by a bureaucracy and by laws; I have no choice in the matter. I can free myself from the power structure to which my birth has chained me, only to find another just as imprisoning in the country that I choose. Because of the stupidity of nationalism, I live in exile on an earth where everything is mine.

"I don't know how to stop the wars." At this time, no matter how much I want to, I haven't a single means to halt the wars that are raging. War, prisons, and closed doors keep me from happiness, even if the victims are thousands of miles away, for if happiness is not shared by all men, it does not exist.

"You can't live if you don't have money." All our lives we are enslaved by money. Even if we live on a farm and raise our own food, this is so. Money corrupts all our relationships with others. But money need not stand between us and the fruits of the earth. We are capable of producing and freely distributing to all everything necessary for life; we are capable of putting an end to competition, overproduction, greed, envy, useless work. The use of money is not a requirement of "human nature." Invented only to simplify barter, it has created an insatiable monster and initiated most crime.

"I am not allowed to smoke marijuana." It is the broad significance of this particular activity that is emphasized here. Society forbids me to extend the frontiers of my consciousness and calls the be-

havior of drug-users antisocial (whereas the drug-
user, in fact, only flees from society on many occasions because the drug has enabled him to see it in
all its horror), while at the same time it decorates
war heroes with medals. Of course, many people do
abuse drugs by taking them without serious intent or
for mere egotistical gratification, as others abuse
alcohol. But the significance of drug use in real life
is that it is one of those acts which automatically
places the offender outside the law, whether he wants
to be or not. It is at this point that he begins to reject society—the society that decides what is good
and bad for him, that legalizes the death of a man
when politics require it and then denies the individual
the means to show that the man's death was assassi-
nation.

"I am not allowed to take my clothes off."
Here is a scandalous absurdity: society forbids me
to show this body of mine, although every human
body is a miracle. Society makes me ashamed of my
body, which must be with me all my life. The
company of the Living Theatre tends to believe that
of the body and the spirit, the body is perhaps the
more beautiful. (Also discernible here is a definite
reaction against the masochistic cult which adulates
supermen with super muscles and Hollywood beau-
ties and regards those who don't fit in it as degener-
ate.) In the myth of Paradise as it is interpreted by
the Christians (among others), the first thing Adam
and Eve do after they eat the fruit is to cover their
bodies, the source of sin. The Puritan imagery says
that they covered first their sexual organs. Everything is organized since childhood, so that the myth
survives, according to the idea that Evil originates
in matter. (This Rite lasts about twenty minutes.)

B. THE VISION OF THE DEATH AND RESUR-
RECTION OF THE AMERICAN INDIAN. After a moment
of silence and motionlessness, the actors gather up
their clothes, throw them in a heap, and mount the

stage. Sitting cross-legged in a circle, they pass a lighted pipe as in an Indian pow-wow. Then they rise, one after another, and stand with heads hanging forward and arms dangling, grouped in five vague formations of four actors each. There is an expectant pause. Then the actors suddenly stand erect like wilted plants responding to rainfall. Each group faces the audience and forms a vertical totem pole of four grimacing faces. (One actor squats down, the second leans over him with his head at the chest level of the third, who supports the fourth on his shoulders.) After freezing for several seconds, they begin to move forward. Then, in rapid sequence, an actor makes the sound of a gunshot and rapidly enacts the brief agony of the bullet's impact before falling face down on the stage. The totem poles are dismantled in an instant.

The Indian council and the totem poles are two symbols that come most easily to mind to represent without set or costumes a once-great culture. In these brief, poignant tableaux the company revives the Indians, whom America massacred by the millions, and demonstrates their speedy destruction by the mere sound of the weapons the white man used. America was founded upon genocide, even if other examples elsewhere in the world are no less ignominious. (The Vision lasts five minutes. Only the stage is lit. The action that follows brings about the Indians' resurrection—the reversal of history.)

C. NEW YORK CITY: EIGHT MILLION PEOPLE ARE LIVING IN A STATE OF EMERGENCY AND DON'T KNOW IT. A voice from among the "dead" Indians on the stage battlefield speaks these words. The prostrate actors then exhort the audience to change the culture by becoming the city of New York. "Be the culture," they say. "Be the police. Show violence. Show anti-violence. Be the forces of repression." Act out the behavior of the guardians of law and order. Feel what it means to be a policeman.

And what is New York? An actor declares, "The island of Manhattan is shaped like a foot.[2] At the foot of New York is Wall Street. Free theatre. In which the actors and the public can do anything they like. (. . .) Do whatever you want with the capitalist culture of New York. Change it. Don't step on the Indians." It is intended that at this moment some members of the audience will come up and remain on stage.

The exhortations continue. "Listen. Under the pavement of New York you can hear the Indians. Enact the culture of New York. Change it." Then: "Form counter-societies. Create a parallel culture." Still prone on the stage, the Indian-actors beat their knees on the boards to represent the vibration of the earth before their revival. The muffled sound creates the expectation of something imminent and unforeseeable. An actor raises his head and begins to chant, "If I could turn you on / If I could drive you out of your wretched mind / If I could tell you / I would let you know." Still chanting, he slowly rises, slapping his thighs in rhythm and starting to dance. The other actors follow, one after another as in a fugue. They scatter among the audience, chanting and dancing for several minutes. The Natural Man, who is able to travel without a passport and do all the other things that were once prohibited, stands up facing the audience.

"Don't step on the Indians." If you wish to come up on the stage, don't hurt the actors: if you want to build a new society, do it in such a way that you don't crush your fellow man, particularly the Natural Man, here represented by the Indian. In

---

[2] The word "foot"—like other words such as legs, hand, sexual revolution, nourishment, heart—on subsequent rungs is a reminder of the part of the Kundalini and Adam Kadmon bodies that corresponds to that rung. We should mention that only excerpts of the actual dialogue spoken by the actors are given. . . . The script in its entirety would take up several dozen pages.

your own fashion, revive the Indian society, the tribe, while preserving the discoveries of science and technology. (The actor speaks here not only as the Indian, but as the nature-sensitive "hippie" and himself as well.)

"If I could drive you out of your wretched mind." By this the actor means to say, "If I, the actor, had the answer, I would give it to you; I wouldn't keep it for myself. But I don't have it. Nothing can replace your own experience." The text of this chant has an authentically revolutionary tenor. Whereas priests have from time immemorial boasted exclusive possession of the secrets that enable them to communicate with the Divinity and thus qualify them as intermediaries between God and the faithful, the Living Theatre company tells the spectator, "We do not have any secrets, but if we had the knowledge that could bring about change, we would communicate it to you at once. We wouldn't fear that you would abuse it." The chant is taken from R. D. Laing's *The Politics of Experience,* one of the texts most frequently referred to by the company.

"I would let you know." This sentence also expresses the actor's intent to establish mutual confidence. The actor has come down from his romantic pedestal. He is naked, prepared to give himself. He has, in effect, already spoken Buber's magic phrase, "I-thou," which is used later on the fifth rung.

Seizing upon a spectator's remark, one actor added to the script, "And how much did you pay to get in?" Admission is charged for the show. It would be, after all, deceptive to give the spectator the impression that theatre can be free in the pre-paradise world. Money must be collected for the simple reason that the actors are forced to insure their subsistence. Marx and Bakunin unquestionably paid their rent but they destroyed in turn, from within, this system in which they were forced to live.

When the actors feel that the improvisation

with the audience has run its course, they begin the Rite of the second Rung.³ Some of them, however, may continue a conversation or action begun with members of the audience. This is done where necessary throughout the performance. When the smaller groups finish their activity, they move on at their own speed to the next stage.

"In order to effect a social change the old values must be replaced or destroyed and either new values set up or an open space of no values created for the wind to blow thru. This destruction of old values is The Revolution of Cultures. This is the work of the Revolutionary at this point in the struggle. It is represented here by the Indians as the Natural Man who serve as examples of tribal and communitarian alternatives, bringing with them the gift of beads and the peace-pipe." (Judith and Julian, written description of *Paradise Now*)

---

³ "Each Rung is an element of a dialectic of Revolution. The first four are steps which culminate in The Revolution of Action, marking the beginning of Anarchist social-restructure and the end of Capitalism and the State. (. . .) The first four Rungs occur (both politically and in the play) in sequence and simultaneously." (Judith and Julian)

33

PARADISE NOW: The Revolution of Revelation

Rung II

A. THE RITE OF PRAYER. Here the actors affirm the sanctity of everything that man's eyes look upon. They are among the audience at the end of Action I and they advance toward the audience and, touching clothing, hair, noses, etc., they proclaim the name of each accompanied by the adjective "holy."

By celebrating the holiness of all things, the company indicates the essential bond that unites all men. They say "holy," not "sacred," rejecting interference by those who would grant themselves the right to decide the sanctity of certain men and objects at the expense of others. Holiness pre-dates the enthronement of priests; it resides in the deepest being of each man and each object that compose the universe. (The Rite lasts about five minutes.)

B. THE VISION OF THE DISCOVERY OF THE NORTH POLE. The light changes to blue and shines on the stage where four actors—two women and two men—stand back to back, facing the four compass points and supporting a fifth on their shoulders. From the audience an actor recites: "This polar expedition took four years to prepare and will take sixteen months to complete. It is one of the most difficult and challenging journeys left to be made by man on this planet." (These lines were taken from a map of the Arctic prepared by the British trans-Arctic expedition of 1968-1969.)

The Pole formed by the five actors starts to

turn, each actor reciting a poem that speaks both of the Pole's physical reality (wind, ice, crevasses) and the relation between the Magnetic Pole and the Revolution. The actors who remained in the audience begin making disjointed movements like crystals come to life. Then, following each other down the aisles, rolling like wheels, they hurl themselves down the corridors of ice toward the Pole. Lining up with the actors on stage, they form three spokes that turn with the Pole in the manner of a large wheel.

As though "charged" with the force emitted by the Pole and flung out by centrifugal force, the actors—the explorers—spin off the spokes, coming to a halt at the edge of the stage. From the Pole issue these questions: "Where are you?" (This is the same first question that God asked Adam.) "How long will you live? What do you want?" The actors answer, "I am here. ("I am ready for God. I am ready to recognize God in this world, I do not hide myself.") "It is time to revolt. To be free," etc. Many of the sequences that follow are already suggested, such as, "After the Revolution, there will be no money," or "To transform the demonic forces into celestial."

(Note that the existence of a personal God is nowhere affirmed in Living Theatre productions. It is not necessary to reascend to God to feel the need to take part in the creative work of the world. It is perhaps the very result of these efforts that we call God. If the world contains God, or if God is but another name for the universe, then "to learn to know God in his madness," another phrase—taken from Brecht's *Antigone*—that refers in Brecht not to the madness of the God Dionysos but of Dryas' son, who rebels against particularly cruel strictures, is seized by Dionysos and stricken insane, may mean here "Dare to face the wrongdoing of men, their acts against life, which have been perpetuated throughout the centuries. If this charnel house Earth reflects Divine nature and Divine qualities, then God is mad.")

The actors who are apparently immobilized in the greatest disarray are actually in predetermined positions. When a voice asks, to characterize all the responses, "What is this called?" the actors leap up and form across the front of the stage the word *ANARCHISM*, each calling out the letter he is forming. Then the voice asks, "What is anarchism?" The actors change formation to the word, *PARA-DISE*, and shout in unison, "Now!"

The discovery made for the audience in the play has for the actors something of the mystery and fascination that surrounded the North Pole at the time when no human being had yet been there. In this Vision, the Pole is a force that attracts crystals to it, melts them, and endows them with an energy that wreaks essential changes in them. (The Vision lasts about five minutes.)

C. BOLIVIA: A GROUP OF REVOLUTIONARIES PLOT THEIR STRATEGY. The blue light disappears. The audience is invited to represent the life of gue-rillas in the Bolivian jungles and the exploitation of man by man in the tin mines. "How strong are your legs? Where are they going? How far will they go?" A voice asks, "Who is the chairman of this clan-destine meeting?"

The object of the Bolivian action is to clarify the destination. Only when this action is actually acted out does Rung II become meaningfully reached. The company suggests non-violent partici-pation in the Bolivian struggle. Why Bolivia? Its interest was topical at the time and suited the play, but other locales are often substituted, such as Prague, Mexico, Madrid, and the various cities where students carrying on their own kind of gue-rilla activity have clashed with the police.

Very often it is at this time that the spectators who have come on stage begin to discuss problems that interest them. No time limit is set, and they may continue as long as they care to.

In the second phase of this Rung, the actors talk about non-violence.

"The Revolution of Revelation describes the aims of the Beautiful Non-Violent Anarchist Revolution. It reveals. It tells what the Revolution is about. It describes another way of being. It creates an atmosphere of Revolution. It speaks of how we can live without money, barter, the state, the police, the armies, and violence. It speaks of a counter-violent strategy. It speaks of what to aim for. It speaks of what to go away from, what to destroy, but, more importantly, of what to create. It makes the destination clear." (Judith and Julian)

34

PARADISE NOW: The Revolution of Gathered Forces

Rung III

A. THE RITE OF STUDY. Seated in yoga position in a spiral formation, the actors trace improvised shapes related to the *mudras*—the hundred or so Tantric gestures of hands and fingers, each of which has a precise meaning—in the air with their arms and hands, drawing on the "energy centers" in their bodies. This ritual generates energy among its participants, which energy here impels each actor to say his lines. The individual actor thus does not know the precise moment that he will speak, for that moment depends upon his reception of the energy released by the *mudras*. The order in which the lines are spoken varies accordingly from performance to performance. The lines are related to the Hindu *mantras,* sacred formulas that must only be pronounced with great concentration. The magic power of words (*savitri*) is considered one of the Sovereign Principles. It is creation by the verb. The *mantras* recited here are all definitions of liberty: "To be free is to be free / of money / of hatred / of punishment / to eat / of prejudice / of violence," etc. When the energy runs out, the actors freeze in their last *mudra.*

Possessing the qualities of both study and communal prayer, this Rite is based on the belief that the word is the source of existence. "The actor pays strict attention to the movements of all the actors within his field of vision. Thus the changing forms and rhythms are never totally the individual's but become communications, the Receptive and the Creative. Therefore it is called the Rite of Study." (Judith and Julian)

Human societies everywhere refer to this belief in their anthropomorphic explanations of Divinity. Even in the Bible, the creations of God are manifested in his Word. God has only to say so for something to exist. The Street Songs in *Mysteries* also draw on this idea. (The Rite lasts about five minutes.)

B. THE VISION OF THE CREATION OF LIFE. The actors rise and the light changes to green. Erect and isolated, they move slowly about the stage, eyes closed. Presently each runs into another, then into a few others, eventually grouping into aggregates of five. Organic life is born amid floating particles. The actors emit a "shhhhhhh" sound and, voluptuously entangled, open their eyes. Then each group raises clasped hands and exults, "Haaaaa. . . ."

Like that of the North Pole, this Vision begins with rigidity. Before coming in contact with each other, the actors are like slivers of ice—blind and possessed of minimal energy. Only when the cell and protoplasm are born does life begin and spread to populate the waters and the earth. Also symbolized here are the helplessness of the individual when alone, and his capability of developing astonishing, joyful creativity when allied with others. (The Vision lasts about six minutes.)

C. (NAME OF LOCALITY) : THERE IS A GROUP OF PEOPLE WHO WANT TO CHANGE THE WORLD. While the preceding rung covered the Revolution of Revelation, this one is addressed to the Revolution of Gathered Forces. By altering the "inner man," the individual has changed his culture and perception and caught a glimpse of the ultimate objective. He must now ally himself with his fellow men and continue the quest with them.

To determine the action on Rung III, the company gathers information on the town in which they are playing, such as the local social problems, strength of the police force, number of prisoners, and types of political groups. Part of the text remains constant: "The hand can gather. The hand can write. The hand can reach." "A basic cell," says Bakunin, "should have five members." The dual meaning of the word "cell" permits the audience to connect the unit of life with the political unit. They are encouraged to peacefully disarm the town's police and its citizens' soul.

The necessity of organization for the Revolution is insisted upon. Who will feed the population and supply it with water and electricity in time of crisis? Discussion of the idea in underground newspapers, leaflets, posters, etc., is urged for all who wish to do so.

"After the culture has been altered and perception changed so that we can see the need for revolution and after The Revolution of Revelation in which the meaning of the revolution has been made clear, people are now ready to gather their forces together and to work together to bring about the Revolution of Action.

"The Revolution of Gathered Forces is not theoretical. Its action consists in consolidating that which is already there.

"Where the Non-Violent ambience is feeble, to strengthen, to support, to teach, to arouse.

"Where there are revolutionaries working for Non-Violent Revolution, to work with them.

"Where the Non-Violent Anarchist Revolution is happening, to support it and to learn from it.

"To initiate PRACTICAL WORK.

"The work of inspiring the uncommitted, of demystifying those caught in the trap of the political myth continues, of course. The primary function of the Revolution of Gathered Forces is to rally those who are ready and to ready those who are open." (Judith and Julian)

35

PARADISE NOW: The Exorcism of Violence and the Sexual Revolution

Rung IV

A. THE RITE OF UNIVERSAL INTERCOURSE. The actors lie on the stage and caress the bodies of those nearest them while the spectators gather around. Then some divide into couples and sit in the position that the Hindus call *maithouna*. Although the couples usually consist of a man and a woman, this is not mandatory. Owing to legal strictures, they do not perform the act of love, but embrace tightly. The stage is suffused with quiet, contemplative joy. In this Rite the company strikes down the barrier of sexual taboo and seeks to demonstrate that every human body is a source of pleasure and beauty. (Though neglected by nearly all revolutionary movements, a sexual revolution, the Becks feel, is essential to man's liberation. The works of Wilhelm Reich and Norman O. Brown on the subject are avidly read by the company.) "Sensation and pleasure are aroused in the genital organs and in the erotic chambers of the mind. Body contact without game playing. The Rite of Prayer, expression of the holiness of all things, is expanded here," as Judith and Julian put it. (All political change is illusory if the mind simply falls back in its old ruts.) Discovery and use of the body, so that feelingful physical awareness can be unified with thought, is an essential Revolutionary Voyage.

B. THE VISION OF APOKATASTASIS. Standing and facing the audience, the actors divide into groups of two, in which one actor plays the executioner and the other the victim. The executioner points his index finger at the victim's temple and makes the sound of a gunshot: "Kch." Twenty times he shoots and each time the victim collapses, then stands up again, hands clasped behind his back. He begins pleading with the executioner, saying, "Holy hand, holy face," etc., but the executioner continues to kill him, answering, "I am not allowed to travel without a passport," etc. Suddenly both stop, recite the words of the Rite of Prayer, begin to touch each other, their faces softening; presently the executioners and victims become embracing couples. Violence has been transformed into anti-violence. A kind of miracle has taken place. At the beginning of the following sequence this miracle will be given the name *apokatastasis*.

When Allen Ginsberg was arrested in the winter of 1967-1968 for civil disobedience during an anti-militarist demonstration, he declaimed poetically: "Pentagon, Pentagon / Reverse consciousness / Apokatastasis." The last word, he explained, meant the transformation of satanic forces into celestial ones.

The Greek word *apokatastasis* means restoration, restitution, re-establishment. It is used by Plato and Plutarch to describe the return of the stars to their original places each year. Politically, it denotes the re-establishment of a former condition. Αποχαταστασις in the Holy Writ and in the writings of the Church Fathers has come to mean both "resurrection" and, what is even more suggestive here, "the restoration of the state of perfection of things as they existed—physically and metaphysically—before the Fall."[1]

The Ginsberg incident brought to the Becks' mind the transformation of the Erinyes to Eumeni-

---

[1] Joseph Henry Trayer, a Greek-English lexicon of the *New Testament*. New York, 1887.

des[2] in Aeschylus' *Eumenides,* although Aeschylus himself never applied the term *apokatastasis* to that transformation in those of his works that have been preserved. Neither is the word mentioned in dictionaries in connection with the Eumenides as dealt with by other writers. It is its early Christian sense that most nearly approaches that used in *Paradise Now*, the only difference being that as far as the Living Theatre is concerned there is neither Fall nor original sin; Paradise is to be created, not its loss mourned.

The company deliberated at considerable length on the way to represent the exorcism of violence on stage. Although we cannot systematically trace the development of this Vision, one of the ideas that the company arrived at in the course of experimentation is worth recounting. They considered presenting from five to fifteen "flashes" of violence in world history, composing a kind of history *mandala.* The first group would have represented war in the forms of Cain / booty: piracy, colonization / religious Crusades / nationalism / nuclear war, and the application of technology to war machines. A second group would have represented sexual oppression as man against woman / goddess with slaves and male sacrifices: matriarchy / man making use of religion to suppress woman / prostitution / and the Hollywood plastic sex image. A third group would have depicted oppression and exploitation: the strong against the weak / Egypt / the building of the pyramids / slave boats, Negroes / genocide—inquisition / and the violent revolutions of slaves.

The ultimate solution was of the utmost simplicity. The elaborate schemes that had been previously envisioned were abandoned in favor of a plan that depicts horror much more clearly. The intolerable repetition of the act of killing alone is what gives the scene its power.

[2] The only example, in all mythologies, of the metamorphosis of evil divinities into good ones.

This representation of massacre by several executioner-victim pairs was inspired by the appalling photograph taken by Edward Adams in Vietnam and published in January, 1968. It showed the chief of the Saigon police holding a pistol to the temple of a captured Vietcong officer in the middle of the street. The expression on the face of the officer about to die was horrifying. The face is nothing but one scream as in the painting by Munch. The photographer got an award. That is just about all that the world did when it saw that picture.

During the performance of this scene, the spectators almost invariably try to stop the massacre by grabbing the arms of the executioners. But the executioners persist unperturbed, occasionally reminding the spectators that one cannot stop violence with violence or reduce the number of times the victim is shot. The spectators are in the end enveloped in the embraces that terminate the scene. ". . . The opponent must be approached with high regard and tenderness and [his] painful motives must be taken into consideration," say the Becks. (The Vision lasts from five to ten minutes.)

C. JERUSALEM: THE VICTIMS BECOME EXECUTIONERS. WHAT DO THE PACIFISTS DO? The audience is invited to put the *apokatastasis* to work in the midst of the Living Theatre's representation of Israeli-Arab conflict. The Jerusalem action thus continues the Rite of Universal Intercourse which, after the *apokatastasis,* may even end with it. "Fuck the Jews. Fuck the Arabs. Fuck means peace," the actors proclaim. In other words, if the Jews and Arabs broke down the touch barrier, there would be no more conflict.

After the *apokatastasis*, the spectators may, if they wish, represent the reversal of history by acting out the end of the violence in Israel. The Jews, persecuted throughout history, have become militarists giving vent to a violence that will eventually turn against them. Will Antigone's warning, "Anyone who uses violence against his enemies will turn and use violence against his own people," be heeded?

The Jerusalem action is the first to be projected into the future, all the others having dealt with the present. The *apokatastasis* has transformed demonic forces into celestial ones. Non-violence is the only means that permits this leap forward in time.

> we cannot
> stop war
> with war
>
> we want
> to get rid of
> coercion
>
> all
> guns
> coerce
>
> . . .
>
> it is 1968
> I am a magic realist[3]

"The fundamental taboo that is channeled into violence is the sexual taboo. To overcome violence we have to overcome the sexual taboo.

"The work of liberation from sexual repression must be a parallel of all revolutionary work and during all revolutionary stages. But there comes a point at which no further progress can be made without abolishing standards that cripple the natural man sexually and this point comes precisely when we confront the fundamental problem of violence.

"The Beautiful Non-Violent Anarchist Revolution will only take place after the Sexual Revolution because before that the energy is violent." (Judith and Julian)

[3] Poem by Julian Beck, published in the London *International Times.*

36

PARADISE NOW: The Revolution of Action

Rung V

A. THE RITE OF THE MYSTERIOUS VOY-
AGE. What happens in this rite is entirely real. In the
center of the circle of actors sits a subject who
undergoes a struggle with demonic forces that he is
allowing to enter him. The surrounding community
of actors does not restrain him, but with cries and
movements of heads and torsos tries to maintain him
in a state of abandon, a self-willed trance. The idea
is that if the community can help the subject boldly
to confront and attack these forces, he will emerge
from the ordeal purified. The company with their
collective energy sustains and propels him in his
struggle against fear and the unknown. The subject
is literally out of his mind, his body wracked by con-
vulsive movements. Some of the spectators are astonished to see the subject and the actors at the end of
the trance radiant, re-charged with energy, and ex-
hibiting joy in voice and gesture.

At the end of the voyage the subject signals to
the rest of the company, physically indicating his
state of being at the moment—how he feels, where
he is at. Several such signals were transmitted in
the course of the first four rungs. (They are spontaneous ones, given as needed, which of course vary
from one evening to the next) There are some also
that happen always at certain places. There is
one, for example, at the end of the Rite of Opposite Forces and the Rite of I and Thou. Judith and
Julian say, "The Signal can be a sound, a word, a
gesture, a look, all or any of these. The Signal is

intended to locate and communicate where the actor is at in relation to himself, his surroundings, the performance, and everyone else. It is usually brief." (The Rite lasts about five minutes.)

B. THE VISION OF THE INTEGRATION OF THE RACES. The light for the *apokatastasis* was pure red. For this Vision it changes to orange. The actors are standing. Suddenly one shouts at another with hatred, "Jew!" The other answers, "Christian!" Two opposing groups form on the stage and advance toward each other. At the moment they meet each is on the defensive, yet almost at the point of giving in. They continue, nevertheless, repeating the process with "Black-white," "young-old," "tall-small." The actors next turn to the audience and shout the same epithets, with a few additions such as "Communist," "SS," etc. Then, alternately pointing to themselves and the spectators, they say, "I-thou; thou-I." The game of superiorities thus ends, and only then.

The idea for this Vision was, of course, provided by Martin Buber's *I and Thou*. According to Buber's philosophy of relation, speaking the words "I-thou," makes impossible the reification of another person, excludes all objectification of the person. He affirms thereby not only his own self-respect, but also the relation with God that is inherent in his relation with the other. On this rung all violence is excluded. Once the sexual revolution is accomplished and constant physical communication among people is established, integration will no longer be a problem. (This Vision lasts five minutes.)

C. PARIS: TIME FUTURE: THE NON-VIOLENT ANARCHIST REVOLUTION. The Paris uprisings of May, 1968, profoundly influenced the Living Theatre, which was in Avignon at the time. France was experiencing a period of hope that can hardly be imagined today, the French having given themselves a new monarch. Judith and Julian happened to be in Paris on business at the most glorious moment. They took part in the seizure of the Odéon, and it was to them that Barrault first addressed himself when he mounted the stage. Julian maintains that the seizure of the Odéon and the events in the former Théâtre de France were the most beautiful acts he had ever seen in any theatre.

Less thrilling days followed. The French went back into their shells, and at Avignon the Living Theatre had to suffer a fascistic backlash along with the despair of the revolutionaries for whom goals were far from clear.

In the Paris Action, the company proposes that the audience finish the Revolution of Paris victoriously. Non-violence is the only key to victory —not cobblestones, not burned cars, but the peaceful occupation of buildings as was done at the Odéon. The time has come not only to allow imagination to take over, but to be finished with the system. "How does it feel to burn money? How do you enact the fall of the state?" asks an actor in a paean to "creative disorder."

Often, spectators burn money then and there, while another part of the audience is usually scandalized and accuses the company of being not logical, although the actors never burn money. This spontaneous act performed by the spectators is characterized by the same invigorating spirit as is being liable to arrest for possession of drugs. It is, after all, no less forbidden to burn the symbol of government gold reserves than it is to drug oneself or undress in public. Burning a bill means much more than simply depriving oneself of its purchasing power. It is a blasphemous act against society; burning money on stage is a revolutionary deed. Paradoxically, it is as if one began feeding every human being; it points to the only possible means of doing so that has nothing to do with charity.

"The Revolution of Action is the turning point between the period of preparatory work and the period of active social restructure. (. . .) It is the work of the actors to guide the public into a projection of the revolutionary situation. (. . .) The Non-Violent Anarchist Revolution means an attempt to live together without punitive law, jails, police, armies, and without the control which money exercises on work, production, and the human character. (. . .) Therefore it cannot be the change imposed by a new ruling class. (. . .) Other incentives will be found. Money puts the State in the position of central control. The hierarchy of money and state can be broken if people could find a way to do without money. Therefore the Revolution of Action is that period during which a significant number of people begin to function without the money system. No barter, no exchange. What is needed can be made and distributed without payment of any sort.

"The Revolution can then create a situation which by virtue of its example will win people over." (Judith and Julian)

37

PARADISE NOW: The Revolution of Transformation

Rung VI

A. THE RITE OF OPPOSITE FORCES. As in the Rite of the Mysterious Voyage, a chosen subject reclines in the center of the circle. For the duration of the Rite his eyes are closed and he is totally relaxed and receptive, breathing slowly and emitting a continuous "Ahhhh. . . ." This sound allows the subject to pass beyond hostile forces and continue his voyage. He is the positive force, while the other actors, though not really negative forces, perform a therapeutic and cathartic function. They grasp and manipulate the subject's body in various manners, sometimes gently, sometimes roughly. He may be hoisted onto an actor's shoulders and worked on aloft by four or five others. The steadiness of the sound he makes is naturally affected according to the treatment he is undergoing.

What happens in this prodigious voyage, anatomically speaking, can be summarized as a deep muscular and respiratory relaxation. The body becomes a furnace of energy; the brain functions with astonishing intensity and freshness, and the subject, who does not know who is doing what to him, feels like an intersection for known and unknown sensations. This Rite is in direct relationship with the definition of the Rung. Images leap into his brain. He banishes the occasional fears that assail him and floats in a sea of happiness. To successfully explore this unknown territory, the actor-therapists must possess an elaborate knowledge of the subject, the characteristics of his body, and his secret energy sources. The techniques range from massage to nibbling, and include stroking him with hair, thumping, and shouting. The subject signals to the other actors when he determines the end of the voyage.

This Rite, referred to by the actors as the "Mat Piece" because they performed it on a straw mattress in Cefalu, was perfected by the troupe through the analysis of different subjects' reactions, and the determination of the most effective methods and optimum duration of each one's voyage. The procedure of the Rite is thus highly dependent on the subject used and whatever else has occurred during a particular evening. The Rite embodies the motif of the Rung—the Revolution of Transformation, the Struggle Period. (The Rite lasts about twelve minutes.)

B. THE VISION OF THE MAGIC LOVE ZAP. This is the only use of the word "magic" in the script of *Paradise Now,* even if a certain magical atmosphere envelops most of the visions—the visions being imaginative expressions of the spiritual elevation attained during the Rite.

Standing and facing outward, the actors link hands in the form of a pentagon. Their fierce facial expressions, raised, menacing arms, the bending of the thighs, and rigid stance imitate certain Oriental demonic statuary and images and the gargoyles of Western cathedrals.

A statue of Mammon composed of three actors supporting two others on their shoulders forms the back wall of the pentagon and looms above the spectators, making jerky, terrifying movements. Slowly, the actors open the pentagon formation to reveal a body stretched out before Mammon. They leap around and fix their eyes on it. From beyond the statue emerge two priests, brandishing an imaginary knife. A great "Rrrrr" is heard and, lifting their feet very high one after another as in Chinese theater, the two priests approach the victim, who braces his body and stretches out his neck to receive the knife. The sight of the victim transforms the executioners. After a moment of paralysis they renounce the sacrifice, gently lowering their arms, while the participating actors relax their hostile expressions. Blackout.

There is powerful contrast between the elaborate build up of the scene and the unexpected brevity of its conclusion. Everything is performed with a calculated rapidity that induces the spectator to wonder, as in the Golem scene in *Frankenstein,* "Am I sure that I didn't dream it?" (The Vision lasts about twenty seconds.)

C. CAPETOWN/BIRMINGHAM ALABAMA: THE BLACKS ARE CONFRONTING THE WHITES WITH REVOLUTION. HOW DO THEY OVERCOME? The lighting was yellow during the Vision. Now the stage is plunged into darkness as the actors recite the theme of the action: Capetown/Birmingham. The heart of darkness. The heart administrates the circulation of the blood. (. . .) Be tender-hearted. Be the great opposing camp. Be the music of Africa." Here the action ordinarily breaks into a rhythmic dance, accompanied by whatever instruments the spectators can employ—hands, feet, voices, seats, drums, tambourines, flutes, etc.[1]

"After The Revolution of Action and The Struggle Period begins, and the reactionary forces confront the revolution with violence, the non-

[1] Sometimes the actions undertaken by the spectators are exclusively a manifestation of physical well-being: music and dance or handclapping. Sometimes they are directly an expression of conflicts, and very theatrical ones, with the use of political invectives and speeches. Even when it is not great one should remember that no other group has ever had such results. *Paradise Now* navigates in a totally unknown territory. No theatre handbook will give the recipes for an intervention of the audience of this kind because it never existed before.

violent revolutionary will confront this destructive force with the strength and meaning of his love force, with the knowledge and wisdom which have become his thru previous revolutionary experience and accomplishment (. . .). And with these he confronts The Great Opposing Camp; and the work of The Revolution now is the transformation of the people of The Great Opposing Camp, and the transformation of the relationship between the revolutionaries of the new society and the militants of the customs of the past. It would have to result, to succeed, to transcend, in the disappearance of enmity." (Judith and Julian)

38 | PARADISE NOW: The Revolution of Being— Glimpses of the Post Revolutionary World

Rung VII

A. THE RITE OF NEW POSSIBILITIES. In the original conception and rehearsals of this Rite, the actors would for five minutes or so emit sounds which they tried to render as unlike human, animal, or electronic sounds as possible done in total darkness. It was exclusively aural, a "sound piece." The company noticed by and by, however, that the sounds weren't audible to the audience, who were preoccupied with producing a semblance of African music. Out of practical considerations, then, it was necessary to eliminate the Rite of New Possibilities, which was really destined for the solitary ear, to condense and integrate it into the Vision that follows.

B. THE VISION OF THE LANDING ON MARS. From the back of the theatre a group of actors, carrying colored flashlights that envelop them in a ghostly glow, advance toward the stage. They are the space ship approaching Mars, and they speak various words and phrases having to do with atoms and the universe, taken at random from an ancient work whose freshness is still undampened, *De Rerum Natura*, Lucretius' atomist-epicurean treatise. Other actors, also bearing colored flashlights, represent the planets, emitting the sounds that formerly accompanied the Rite. One actor borne about by others represents a faraway galaxy. He is adorned with tiny white lights on the ankles, knees, navel, elbows, hands, and forehead, and writhes about in slow motion with spread legs and open arms, balancing very slowly.

The Rite and Vision are images of the discoveries that await man beyond known space after the Revolution. They concern the unknowable, the unthinkable. The Rung is called Glimpses of the Post Revolutionary World.

Why Mars? Because it is the goal of every childhood dream of outer space. Of all the creatures that might appear from space it is the Martians who have intrigued men most, even more than, say, the moonmen, the Selenites. To the popular imagination, Mars is the most mysterious of planets.

There is no terror, however, in this Vision. The post-revolutionary world will make expeditions of this kind possible. What will we do? We will discover. (The Vision lasts about five minutes.)

C. HANOI/SAIGON: THERE IS A GROUP LIVING IN AN ANARCHIST SOCIETY. WHAT ARE THEY DOING? Here we are in the midst of the unimaginable: Hanoi and Saigon are not only reconciled, but have become a part of a world where anarchy has triumphed. "No money. No laws. No bureaucracy. Breathe. Get high. Fly. In heaven they teach you to breathe."

In the Avignon performances, the exhortations "Breathe, fly" were matched by stage action of equivalent "madness." The actors, accompanied by willing spectators, would climb to a window of the Carmelite Cloister—a section of ruined wall—and after taking several deep breaths throw themselves into the air like birds taking flight, eyes on the sun. Two rows of actors below caught the flyers in a network of clasped arms. The idea bore such positive results that it was kept in later performances, with a table or step ladder substituting for the wall.

What makes the flying act so conclusively forceful is its intimate relation with the theme of this Rung: throwing oneself down requires absolute confidence in those below. When the leaper is caught, he is laid on the ground beneath the interlaced arms, to make room for the next. (The leap itself was borrowed from choreographer Anne Halprin.)

"The economic, political and social changes effected by the Revolution of Action in addition to all of the anterior changes effected in our character during all the preceding revolutionary stages must influence the development of human potential. When our relationship to the world and to ether, to our environment and to ourselves, to work and to time, to science and to nature, have been freed from the constraint and injury brought down on us by the errors of the past civilization, we will be freer to expand and to alter the nature of our being." (Judith and Julian)

39

PARADISE NOW: The Permanent Revolution. Change!

Rung VIII

A. THE RITE OF I AND THOU. In a motif inspired by the Tibetan *Book of the Dead*, the actors go through the act of dying, being reborn, and forming the tree of knowledge. They speak the word "Om" and follow it with a gloomy "Rrr. . . ." inhaling as deeply as possible. The five stages in this voyage are 1) weakening; 2) feeling death seize the throat, change of breathing; 3) feeling the arrest of cell renewal by oxygen combustion, disintegration of being; 4) loss of vision (the eyes film over); 5) taking leave of the world.

When an actor nears death's door, he signals to the others the degree of his fright and his state of mind and receives their signals in return. Then couples form, the actors touch each other, the sound changes, and life is reborn in the exchange of energies. The actors leave death's door to construct the tree of knowledge.

B. THE VISION OF UNDOING THE MYTH OF EDEN. The tree of knowledge is formed with three men and two women supported on the shoulders of other actors, the group of couples encircled by the rest of the troupe. The tree speaks. In rapid summary it runs through, in order, all the prominent phrases, gestures, and sounds of the previous acts, reproducing the tone of each Rite, Vision, and Action, and recalling all the knowledge accumulated in the course of the evening. In *Genesis* there are two different trees. The tree of life, in the middle of the garden, and the tree of knowledge of good and evil. God says to Adam not to eat the fruit of the tree of knowledge because he will die if he does. The serpent promises Adam he will, on the contrary, become as wise as God. This could be possible if Adam would eat the fruit of the tree of knowledge and then become immortal by eating the fruit of the tree of life. But God puts at the gates celestial beings with flaming swords to keep Adam away from the tree of life.

In *Paradise Now*, unlike *Genesis*, the actors represent the tree of knowledge without distinguishing it from the tree of life. They do not reject the spectator who tastes the first fruit. Instead they open a horn of plenty: the circle around the tree opens and the actors spill out into the audience, mingling with the people, and conducting them out of the theatre into the street.

C. THE STREET. There are no archangels at the door to this Paradise. What the brain acquires through study intervenes in life. (The Living Theatre preserves the vision of Paradise, but renounces the myth of Eden.) The jubilation that infects the spectators and actors at this point was most manifest in the incredible procession that followed the second performance of *Paradise Now* at Avignon. It ended at close to two in the morning. In the street, spectators surrounded the actors in a compact circle of about two hundred people. An intense bond of communication united them, despite the fact that most of them did not know each other. A humming sound rose spontaneously from the crowd, and as if propelled by an invincible force, it split into ranks and with linked arms marched the length of two long streets before breaking up in front of the Cloister.

Some of these spectators decided to embark on the quest for the Paradise, which is earthly, yet without limits. For the true Revolution is permanent and the only boundary of the voyage they would undertake is their physical departure from this earth.

40

AVIGNON: EXIT

The procession just described was not regarded with pleasure by everyone. It was, in fact, one of the indirect causes of the Living Theatre's departure from Avignon.

Because of the revolutionary events of May, out of the five troupes scheduled for the Festival, only the Béjart and the Living Theatre were in Avignon. They found themselves caught in between the aspirations of the May combatants and the suppression of all organized cultural demonstrations. The political atmosphere of Avignon itself, moreover, was tense. Deputy Mayor Henri Duffaut, in office for six years, was under pressure to retire. His opponent, Jean-Pierre Roux, made use of the Living Theatre as a weapon. In an attack on the mayor he wrote, "Who receives, who nurtures those bums, those Freudians of the Living Theatre whose immorality is an offense to our youth and our workers?" The daily *Le Méridional* adopted a tone equally ignoble: " ... the Avignonnais are shocked by the behavior, clothed or unclothed, of this beast." The columnist closed with the malediction, "Avignon, Avignon, your Festival has diarrhea." The Living Theatre was thus under attack by both enemies of the Avignon Festival and defenders of the traditions of the City of Popes.

On the day of the premiere of *Paradise Now*, *Le Méridional* ran another gem of an article: "They [the citizens of Avignon] hold fast to their tranquillity, to the poetry of their streets, to the calm of their ancient, charming neighborhoods, to their Festival—provided that this Festival, like its predecessors, serves the glory of France, Avignon, and our great tongue, and continues to draw tourists to the City of Popes, well known for her graciousness." Wednesday, July 24, was the premiere; Thursday the 25th saw the second performance (followed by the procession in the streets). On Friday the 26th, the city obtained a court summons demanding the withdrawal of the play for disturbing the peace. The summons did not arrive until the next day, and *Paradise Now* was performed on Friday for the third and last time in Avignon.

On Saturday afternoon, Judith and Julian had an interview with the mayor. The mayor, speaking for the city, ordered the Living Theatre to substitute either *Mysteries* or *Antigone* for *Paradise Now* for the five remaining performances. Julian counterproposed to continue *Paradise Now* but to change the street scene.

Too late, replied the mayor. He further denied the Becks' request to give free open-air performances since all Festival tickets were sold and spectators had to be turned away. An order would be issued to this effect. Judith and Julian left the mayor without promising to strike *Paradise Now* from the bill; they wanted to discuss the matter with their actors. The same evening Julian went to Central Square in the Cité Louis-Gros district—the workers' district—where a free show was to be offered the following Friday. He spoke about the procession: "It was a peaceful march, a manifestation of radiant joy. The sounds emitted by the people tried to transform in the city the vibrations of violence, of hatred, of hostility, of alienation into friendly ones."

Meanwhile, the mayor held a press conference, and the Sunday morning papers carried a varied array of stories. According to *Le Méridional*, the mayor said, "We have met with Mr. Julian Beck and held a discussion with him. He declared that he has decided not to perform *Paradise Now*, nor to give street performances." This sensational news item graced the front page.

La Marseillaise noted that the mayor regarded himself as a "customer cheated by a piece of merchandise that did not conform to his specifications." More honest was *Le Dauphiné Libéré,* which reported that "the Living Theatre promised to consult its actors on the subject of *Paradise Now,* but did not reveal whether or not it would present another play in its place."

The Living Theatre did indeed consult its actors. At six-thirty p.m., in the orchard of Pope Urban V, Julian read the following announcement:

STATEMENT OF THE LIVING THEATRE

The Living Theatre has decided to withdraw from the Festival d'Avignon

1. Because, without using the word interdiction, all further performances of *Paradise Now* have been forbidden by the city in collaboration with the Administration of the Festival, under threat of repressive action and legal procedings.

2. Because the patron of the Festival, the Mayor of Avignon, in collaboration with the Administration of the Festival, has forbidden all free performances in the streets of Avignon, although all tickets for the Festival have already been sold; and because they, the patrons of the Festival, state categorically that they do not believe that the people are entitled to the theatre unless they can pay for it.

3. Because we have a choice between being dictated to by a Municipality and Festival Administration, which wish under pretext to suppress our free expression as

artists, and between working for our own liberty and that of other people.

4. Because we have a choice between bowing down to a command disguised as a request, between accepting broken contractual terms, or withdrawing from a Festival which wishes to stop us from playing what we are contracted to play.

5. Because we wish to choose the solution which will lessen the violence in this city.

6. Because you cannot serve God and Mammon at the same time, you cannot serve the people and the state at the same time, you cannot serve liberty and authority at the same time, you cannot tell the truth and lie at the same time, you cannot play *Antigone* (which is about a girl who refuses to obey the arbitrary dictates of the state and performs a holy act instead) and at the same time substitute *Antigone* in the place of a forbidden play.

7. Because the time has come for us at last to begin to refuse to serve those who do not want the knowledge and power of art to belong to any but those who can pay for it, who wish to keep the people in the dark, who work for the Power Elite, who wish to control the life of the artist and the lives of the people.

8. Because the time has come to liberate art and to remove its support from the Age of Humiliation and Exploitation.

9. Because the time has come to say No before our last shreds of honor are lost.

10. Because our art cannot be used any longer to represent authorities whose actions oppose what we believe in.

11. Because, although it does not please

us to lean on the justice of the law, we are convinced that our legal rights have been imposed on and broken, and that therefore we have been freed by this rupture to take this necessary action.

The Company of the Living Theatre
Avignon, 28 July 1968

41

NEW YORK (COMEBACK)

In spite of this declaration and the fact that the Living Theatre chose to leave the Festival, it has been said that the company was expelled, as it was said they were expelled from the States. Neither is true. There was, however, a painful scene when the group left Avignon. The police violently evicted the actors from their quarters. Said Jean Vilar: "It was a clumsy and inhuman gesture." On Sunday, the 4th of August, Vilar and Béjart offered the people precisely what the Living Theatre was not allowed to do: a free performance! A gigantic dinner was served and the Béjart dancers performed. It looked a little strange after what had just happened. In the weeks following, the Living Theatre gave a free performance of *Paradise Now* in Ollioules, and five consecutive ones in Geneva at the Palais des Sports before embarking on the S.S. *Aurelia* for the United States on August 31, 1968.

From 1964 to 1968 the troupe had not been back to New York. Still, the company always affirmed that they would return to America if offered a contract that included a round-trip ticket. In 1968 the Radical Theatre Repertory, an organization composed of some twenty "marginal" American troupes, met these conditions and organized an American tour for the Living Theatre, who, used to European arrangements and distances and after such a long absence, would hardly have known how to go about it themselves. From September, 1968, to March, 1969, the troupe traveled some 18,000 miles back and forth across the United States, playing *Paradise Now,*

Antigone, Frankenstein, and *Mysteries.* It is still too soon to evaluate the results of the tour. We will only say that, contrary to the predictions of critics who thought American theatre "much more advanced," the Living Theatre made an extraordinary impression both in New York and in small towns where they were completely unknown. The *Village Voice* named *Frankenstein* among the best plays of the season and conferred awards on Judith and Julian for their interpretations in *Antigone.* (The Living Theatre's acceptance-telegram read, in part: "The theatre is life and the theatre is in the street. The problem the theatre has to solve today is its transformation from a theatre of violence and cruelty into a theatre of freedom and joy. (. . .)"

The zigzag touring was exhausting, however, and money was sometimes short. As a result, the troupe was not able to get a new show on the boards. They did present, however, an interesting variation of *Paradise Now.* Booked at several colleges and universities under the reassuring designation of "lecture-demonstration," the troupe would enter the hall where the students were assembled and perform the Rite of Guerilla Theatre, much to everyone's surprise. Instead of ending by undressing, they sat down on the stage. Julian, with the help of a few actors, would describe what they had just done, explain the reasons for the choice of one phrase over another, and comment on the acting technique. Very lively discussions often followed, leading sometimes to argument. Occasionally the actors would remember a spectator's reactions during the scene and get him to explain himself. Then Julian would invite willing spectators to take the place of the actors and interpret the Rite for their fellow students. An actor obligingly recited the phrases. During the fifth phrase, all the actors would silently disappear from the room and leave the student-actors, still shouting out their frustration, face to face with their comrades, alone with their shouting, their roles, their suffering. A palpably different feeling would unite the assembly. They had to continue; it was no longer an act. The word theatre suddenly didn't mean the same any more. The impromptu students found themselves in the midst of everyday drama.

Another singular and memorable event that equaled the notorious evening of the Free Theatre in Milan befell the troupe just before they left the States. It was a confrontation organized by the Theatre of Ideas, a society (not a theatre) that arranges meetings and debates for its members with invited guests of the caliber of, say, Norman Mailer or Herbert Marcuse. On March 21st, the group invited four special guests for an evening entitled "Theatre OR Therapy?": the critic Robert Brustein, Chairman of the Yale University Drama Department and proponent of an esthetic theory of theatre (the theatre can't change the world and doesn't have to try to change it), Judith Malina, Julian Beck, and the Becks' old anarchist friend, Paul Goodman. The adversaries were seated facing the audience on two benches, separated by a moderator. It cost $10 to attend, and the gathering included film director Arthur Penn, writers Susan Sontag and Norman Mailer, and various other members of the New York intelligentsia.

The actors of the Living Theatre were not invited, but they showed up anyway, in the middle of Robert Brustein's remarks, and insisted on being admitted. Whenever Brustein's ideas seemed too reactionary to them, they did not hesitate to say so at the top of their voices.

Goodman, who confessed to not having seen any of the company's latest shows, launched into a bold defense of their classicism, invoking their productions of *Phèdre,* Pirandello, etc. Judith spoke, calling upon anarchist principles, and evoked an actor's retort to Brustein's assertion that the theatre is composed of supremely gifted people: "We are all supremely gifted people, every human being." Actor

Jim Tiroff—black glasses, orange cape, violet plumes, a cigar—stood provocatively in front of the audience, who began to get annoyed. They wanted the discussion to continue. Far from deploring the scene, Judith asked the audience "Why are you so easily upset?" She was visibly delighted by the stir created by the troupe; something was happening—why stick to the program? Goodman became angry and left, despite Julian's attempts to detain him. The hostess took the microphone and apologized profusely for the frightful disturbance. The room began to look more and more like the stage of *Paradise Now*. Members of the audience left their places and probing conversations sprang up everywhere. Using techniques perfected in *Paradise Now*, the actors virtually exploded the gathering. Norman Mailer could not manage to be taken seriously. Judith called after those who were leaving, "Don't give up so soon!"

Judith and Julian were pressed for a disavowal of what had taken place—the last thing they wanted to give. Neither of them had had any knowledge of the troupe's intentions, and nothing had been prepared or decided in advance; but there was pride in Judith's and Julian's eyes.

The assemblage gradually shed its reserve and people were seizing the microphone. An elderly gentleman proclaimed that he had just witnessed the death of civilization, a lady stated that troublemakers ought to be whipped, and a young man appealed to "Shakespeare's spirit." The once polite gathering, in which no one had had the courage to behave according to his beliefs, was suddenly transformed into an open forum. "Stop analyzing, start living!" urged Rufus Collins. Judith added, "Don't vote any more. Speak to each other. Let people talk to one another." Many members of the company took the opportunity to announce their particular grievances, such as the black problem, American liberalism, the war, etc. One man told the actors as he was leaving, "I've changed my mind. I love you."

At two in the morning, after five hours of heated debate, when the last actors and participants had gone, a single couple remained in the room: an undernourished young man without a shirt and a severely dressed gray-haired woman in her fifties clasped in a long, passionate embrace.

42

A NON-CONCLUSION
OF SORTS

In the summer of 1969, the company was in Morocco to work on a collective production. But this time there were new problems to be solved, new questions to be answered: Would the Living Theatre remain content filling contractual obligations, as invitations from all over Europe continued to arrive in a steady stream? What exactly would be the company's role in the Revolution? Would they keep on performing in theatres for that segment of the public that has access to cultural events? What about the "non-public"—a term coined in France after the events of May, 1968? Would the Living Theatre bear without flinching the accusations of students to the effect that the troupe is fundamentally a product coopted by the bourgeois culture?

In the face of these pressing problems, no headway was being made on the new production. Each day, meetings dealt with the fundamentals of the company's existence and future, instead. The Moroccan summer passed as the once collective creativity was channeled into different energies.

On the boat between Spain and Naples an historic meeting took place. When all passengers were already asleep the actors talked about change. No decision was made that night but when Capri emerged from the dark night everybody knew that this day was a special one. The metamorphosis had started.

By the time the troupe began its Italian tour, it was becoming clear that the Living Theatre was no longer what it once was, nor would it ever be. Throughout the Italian tour, discussion continued about decentralization and diversification—the two focal concepts of future operations. True to the millennial tradition, the gypsy tribe was about to divide into separate family groups.

On January 11, 1970, *Mysteries* was performed for the last time in the Akademie der Künste in Berlin. The body pile was heavier than usual. Twenty-one corpses. In the furnace, in the grave. It was important to die correctly. In order to be reborn. . . . Two months later, the underground press and the principal news media of the West received the following announcement:

LIVING THEATRE ACTION DECLARATION

January, 1970

The structure is crumbling. All of the institutions are feeling the tremors. How do you respond to the emergency?

For the sake of mobility the Living Theatre is dividing into four cells. One cell is currently located in Paris and the center of its orientation is chiefly political. Another is located in Berlin and its orientation is environmental. A third is located in London and its orientation is cultural. A fourth is on its way to India and its orientation is spiritual. If the structure is to be transformed it has to be attacked from many sides. This is what we are seeking to do.

In the world today there are many movements seeking to transform this structure—the Capitalist-Bureaucratic-Military-Authoritarian-Police Complex —into its opposite: a Non-Violent-Communal-Organism. The structure will fall if it's pushed the right way. Our purpose is to lend our support to all the forces of liberation.

But first we have to get out of the trap. Buildings called theatres are an architectural trap. The man in the street will never enter such a building.

1. Because he can't: The theatre buildings belong to those who can afford to get in; all buildings are property held by the Establishment by force of arms.
2. Because the life he leads at work and out of work exhausts him.
3. Because inside they speak in a code of things which are neither interesting to him nor in his interest.

The Living Theatre doesn't want to perform for the privileged elite anymore because all privilege is violence to the underprivileged.

Therefore the Living Theatre doesn't want to perform in theatre buildings anymore. Get out of the trap; the structure is crumbling.

The Living Theatre doesn't want to be an institution anymore. It is out front clear that all institutions are rigid and support the Establishment. After twenty years the structure of the Living Theatre had become institutionalized. All the institutions are crumbling. The Living Theatre had to crumble or change its form.

How do you get out of the trap?

1. Liberate yourself as much as possible from dependence on the established economic system. It was not easy for the Living Theatre to divide its community, because the community was living and working together in love. Not dissension, but revolutionary needs have divided us. A small group can survive with cunning and daring. It is now for each cell to find means of surviving without becoming a consumer product.
2. Abandon the theatres. Create other cirmustances for theatre for the

man in the street. Create circumstances that will lead to Action, which is the highest form of theatre we know. Create Action.

3. Find new forms. Smash the art barrier. Art is confined in the jail of the Establishment's mentality. That's how art is made to function to serve the needs of the Upper Classes. If art can't be used to serve the needs of the people, get rid of it. We only need art if it can tell the truth so that it can become clear to everyone what has to be done and how to do it.

APPENDIX I

A. PRODUCTIONS STAGED BY THE LIVING THEATRE IN NEW YORK

At the Becks' apartment, 789 West End Avenue:
Childish Jokes by Paul Goodman; *Ladies' Voices* by Gertrude Stein; *He Who Says Yes and He Who Says No* by Bertolt Brecht; *The Dialogue of the Mannequin and the Young Man* by Federico Garcia Lorca. August 15, 1951.

At the Cherry Lane Theatre, 38 Commerce Street:
Doctor Faustus Lights the Lights by Gertrude Stein (December 2, 1951).

Beyond the Mountains by Kenneth Rexroth (December 30, 1951).

An Evening of Bohemian Theatre: *Desire Trapped by the Tail* by Pablo Picasso; *Ladies' Voices* by Gertrude Stein; *Sweeney Agonistes* by T. S. Eliot (March 2, 1952).

Faustina by Paul Goodman (May 25, 1952).

Ubu the King by Alfred Jarry; *The Heroes* by John Ashbery (August 5, 1952).

At the Loft, Broadway and 100th Street:
The Age of Anxiety by W. H. Auden (March 18, 1954).

The Spook Sonata by August Strindberg (June 3, 1954).

Orpheus by Jean Cocteau (September 30, 1954).

The Idiot King by Claude Fredericks (December 2, 1954).

Tonight We Improvise by Luigi Pirandello (February 17, 1955).

Phèdre by Jean Racine (May 27, 1955).
The Young Disciple by Paul Goodman (October 12, 1955).

At the Living Theatre, 14th Street and Sixth Avenue:

Many Loves by William Carlos Williams (January 13, 1959).
The Cave at Machpelah by Paul Goodman (June 30, 1959).
The Connection by Jack Gelber (July 15, 1959).
Tonight We Improvise by Luigi Pirandello (November 6, 1959).
The Theatre of Chance: I. *The Marrying Maiden* by Jackson MacLow; II. *The Women of Trachis* by Ezra Pound, after Sophocles (June 22, 1960).
In the Jungle of Cities by Bertolt Brecht (December 20, 1960).
The Apple by Jack Gelber (December 7, 1961).
Man Is Man by Bertolt Brecht (September 18, 1962).
The Brig by Kenneth H. Brown (May 15, 1963). After the seizure of the 14th Street Theater this play continued its run at the Midway Theater on West 42nd Street for two months.[1]

B. FILMS BASED ON LIVING THEATRE PRODUCTIONS

The Connection directed and edited by Shirley Clarke. Screenplay by Jack Gelber, based on his play; camera, Arthur J. Ornitz; sets, Richard Sylbert; costumes, Ruth Morley; music, Freddie Redd. The following members of the company ap-

---

[1] The dates printed in Kenneth H. Brown, *The Brig,* are inexact. They have been corrected here. To be complete we should add that the Living Theatre played also Pirandello's *Giants of the Mountain* at the 14th Street theatre. It was given four times for the Pirandello Society. Geraldine Lust directed it.

peared in the film: Warren Finnerty, Garry Goodrow, Jerome Raphael, Carl Lee, Jim Anderson, Barbara Winchester, Henry Proach. Allen-Hogdon Productions, 1960, in black and white. (The Becks had no control over the production, which was in the hands of Shirley Clarke, a former ballerina. It was her first feature-length film and she financed it by selling 250 shares, which ranged in value from $50 to $5,000. In this way, she retained creative control without interference from investors. Despite the film's critical success, a peculiar financial arrangement whereby the Living Theatre had to pay its actors scale salaries for five weeks, according to Equity rules, no matter how long the shooting would be, resulted in heavy losses for the company. It has so far received $2,500 in royalties, having paid out $5,000 in salaries.)

The Brig, directed by Jonas and Adolfas Mekas. Screenplay by Kenneth H. Brown, based on his play; produced by David C. Stone for White Line Productions, 1964, 68 minutes in black and white. (Jonas Mekas shot the film on the stage of the Midway Theatre in a matter of hours at a cost of $800. They had full cooperation from the Becks, who are very fond of the film. In contrast to the financial arrangements of *The Connection,* the company has been receiving regular, appreciable royalty payments from the producers of this enterprise.)

Who's Crazy? written and directed by Allan Zion and Tom White. Produced by Cinemasters International, 1965, in black and white. The cast consists of seventeen members of the company. (The film was shot in twelve days in Heist-sur-Mer in January, 1965, while the Becks were in prison. The Becks found the script very weak and tried to prevent the production of the film, but the company was in such dire straits that they allowed production to go ahead in the hope of making money out of it. The film was a disaster, both artistically and financially. It was shown once at the Locarno Festival in 1965 but never distributed.)

In addition to the above, a number of films featured individual members of the company, and others used the company in toto. John Huston used the troupe for a short scene in *The Bible* in 1965; in the same year several members had parts in an Italian film, *Io, Io, Io . . . E Gli Altri*, which starred Gina Lollobrigida and Vittorio de Sica and was directed by the veteran Alessandro Blasetti. Also *Candy*, Christian Marquand's notorious creation, used the company in a very brief scene; Julian Beck had a role in Pier Paolo Pasolini's *Edipo Re*; and Judith Malina, Luke Theodore, and Mary Mary had small roles in Peter Goldman's *Wheel of Ashes*. Alfredo Leonardi made a short documentary in Rome in 1965, *Living and Glorious*, based on excerpts from *The Brig* and *Mysteries* and including brief scenes of the company's life in Rome. The same Leonardi used the entire company in his first feature-length film in 1966, *Amore, Amore*. In 1967, the company performed a very remarkable sketch ("Agony") by Bernardo Bertolucci in an Italian episodic film, *Vangelo 70,* which contained sketches by Godard and Pasolini, among others. In 1968, a Dutch film, *Le Compromis,* featured scenes from *Mysteries* and *Antigone* as parts of its plot.

C. TELEVISION SHOWS BASED ON LIVING THEATRE PRODUCTIONS

UNITED STATES: On August 2, 1964, a scene from *The Brig* was telecast on the CBS program "Look Up and Live." During the company's 1968-1969 tour, CBS taped several scenes from various performances, and on March 8, 1969, WQED in San Francisco telecast scenes from *Mysteries*.

EUROPE: *The Brig*, Berlin, November 1, 1964;

Frankenstein, Berlin, October 17, 1965; *Mysteries,* Copenhagen, December 30, 1965; *The Maids,* Amsterdam, December 6, 1966; *Mysteries,* Laren, Holland, December 12, 1966; *Mysteries,* Paris, October 13, 1967; interviews and excerpts from *Frankenstein, Mysteries, Antigone,* Lausanne, taped by BBC in January, 1968; Improvisation on the Theme: *Withdraw the Troops From Vietnam and the World,* London, taped in June, 1969, BBC.

D. RECORDINGS

Music from *The Connection,* Freddie Redd Quartet; Blue Note LP #4027.

Music from *The Connection* by Freddie Redd, performed by the Howard McGhee Quintet; London LTZ-U 15221, mono.

Le Living Theatre: Paradise Now, recorded during performance in Geneva, August 24, 1968; Nili Productions, distributed by Bam, 133 Bvd. de Raspail, Paris, VIe.

Dialectics of Liberation includes a speech by Julian Beck on the subject, "Money, Sex, and the Theatre," along with addresses by R. D. Laing, Herbert Marcuse, Allen Ginsberg, Stokely Carmichael, *et al.* Intersound Recordings Ltd., Liberation Records, 20 Fitzroy Sq., London W1.

E. SELECTED BIBLIOGRAPHY

1. General works on the American theatre that include discussions of the Living Theatre: *Theatre USA 1668 to 1957* by Bernard Hewitt, New York: McGraw-Hill, 1959. *Le Théâtre aux États-Unis* by F. Kourilsky (in French), Brussels: Renaissance du Livre, 1967. *Panorama du Théâtre Américain* by L. Villard (in French), Paris: Seghers, 1964. *Seasons of Discontent* by Robert Brustein, New York: Simon & Schuster, 1965.

2. Works about specific productions of the Living Theatre in America: "The Living Theatre" by W. Glover, *Theatre Arts* Vol. XLV, No. 12, December,

1961. "Where There Is Total Involvement" by **R.** Hatch, *Horizon* Vol. IV, No. 4, March, 1962. "The New American Theatre" by R. Kostelanetz, *Stand* Vol. VI, No. 4, June, 1964. "Theatre of God" by K. Brown, *Plays and Players* Vol. XI, No. 12, September, 1964.

3. About the American tour of 1968-1969: PE-RIODICALS: *Yale/Theatre* Vol. II, No. 1, special issue devoted to the LT, Spring, 1969. "The Return of the Living Theatre" in *The Drama Review* Vol. XIII, No. 3, Spring, 1969. "Le Living" by S. Schneck, *Ramparts*, November 30, 1968. "The Final Decline and Total Collapse of the American Avant-Garde" by E. Lester, *Esquire,* May, 1969. "Monkey Business" by R. Brustein, *New York Review of Books,* April 24, 1969. BOOKS: *The Living Theatre USA,* by Renfrew Neff, New York and Indianapolis: The Bobbs-Merrill Co., 1970; *We, The Living Theatre,* by Aldo Rostagno and Gianfranco Mantegna with Julian Beck and Judith Malina, New York: Ballantine Books, Inc., 1970.

4. Writings by Judith Malina and Julian Beck: "Last Performance at the Living Theatre Invective" by J. Malina, *Evergreen Review* No. 33, August-September, 1964. "How to Close a Theatre" by J. Beck, *Tulane Drama Review* Vol. VIII, No. 3, Spring, 1964. "Thoughts on Theatre from Jail" by J. Beck, *The New York Times*, February 21, 1965. *The Brig*: A Concept for Theatre or Film (with an essay on the Living Theatre by J. Beck and Director's Notes by J. Malina) by K. H. Brown, New York: Hill & Wang, 1965. "Notes on the Direction of *Frankenstein*" by J. Beck, *City Lights Journal,* No. 3, 1966. *Living Theatre Poems*, New York: Boss Books, 1968.

APPENDIX II

A. EUROPEAN TOURS OF THE LIVING THEATRE

1961

June:

Rome, Teatro Parioli: *The Connection; Many Loves*
Turin, Teatro Carignano: *The Connection*
Milan, Piccolo Teatro: *The Connection; Many Loves*
Paris, Théâtre des Nations, Vieux-Colombier: *The Connection; Many Loves; In the Jungle of Cities*
Berlin, Akademie der Künste: *The Connection; Many Loves*
Frankfort, Schauspielhaus: *The Connection*

1962

April, May:

Paris, Théâtre de Lutèce: *The Connection; The Apple; In the Jungle of Cities*
Zürich, Schauspielhaus: *The Connection*
Düsseldorf, Kammerspiele: *The Connection; In the Jungle of Cities*
Maastricht, Stadsschouwburg: *The Connection*
Amsterdam, Petite Comédie: *The Connection*
Rotterdam, De Lantaarn: *The Connection*
Eindhoven, Philips Memorial Theater: *The Connection*

Scheveningen, Kurhaus Paviljoen: *The Connection*
Nijmegen, Stadsschouwburg: *The Connection*
Antwerp, Opéra: *The Connection*
Brussels, Palais des Beaux Arts: *The Apple; The Connection*

1963—No tour.

1964

September 2-26, London, Mermaid Theatre: *The Brig* (43—two performances each evening)
October 26, Paris, American Students and Artists Center: *Mysteries* (1) Opening
November 2-7, Brussels, Théâtre 140: *The Brig* (5)
    6, Antwerp, Arenlorg Schouwburg: *The Brig* (1)
    9, Basel, Komödie: *The Brig* (1)
    19, Berlin, Akademie der Künste: *The Brig* (1)

1965

February 5-13, Brussels, Théâtre 140: *Mysteries* (10)
    15-16, Amsterdam, Théâtre Carré: *Mysteries* (2)
    17, Rotterdam, De Lantaarn: *Mysteries* (1)
    26-March 12, Berlin, Forum Theater: *Maids* (16) Opening.
March 12-14, Rome, Eliseo: *Mysteries* (3)
    16-18, Turin, Gobbetti: *The Brig* (3)
    26-28, Rome, Parioli; *The Brig* (3)
April 9-13, Rome, Teatro dei Satiri: *Mysteries* (5)
    14, Naples, San Fernandino: *Mysteries* (1)
    15-22, Rome, Teatro dei Satiri: *Mysteries* (7)
    23, Trieste, Teatro Stabile: *Mysteries* (1) The performance for April 24th was canceled by the police.
    28-May 2, Florence, Teatro di San Apollonio: *Mysteries* (4)
May 15-16, Naples, San Fernandino: *The Brig* (2)

June 18-24, Berlin, Akademie der Künste: *Mysteries* (7)

July 6-17, Berlin, Forum Theater: *Maids* (13) Two performances on July 12.

23-25, Munich, Theater in der Leopoldstrasse: *Maids* (4)

26-August 1, *The Brig* (5)

August 2 and 5, *Mysteries* (2)

3-4, *Maids* (2)

September 25-27, Venice, Teatro La Perla: *Frankenstein* (3) Press preview, September 25; official opening September 26.

October 15-17, Berlin, Akademie der Künste: *Frankenstein* (3)

21, Stuttgart, Kammertheater: *Maids* (1)

22, *Mysteries* (1)

23, Bremen, Theater der Freien Hansestadt: *Mysteries* (1)

25, Soest (Germany), Wilhelm Morgner Haus: *Maids* (1)

November 2, Cologne, Schauspielhaus: *The Brig* (1)

4, Rolandseck, Bahnhof (train station): *Mysteries* (1)

6, *Maids* (1)

8-9, Frankfort, Intercontinental Hotel: *Maids* (2); *Mysteries* (2)

10, Mühlheim-Cologne, Stadthalle: *Maids* (1); *Mysteries* (1)

13, Bonn, Universität Hörsaal: *Mysteries* (1)

15, Aachen, Technische Universität, Grosser Hörsaal: *Maids* (1)

19, Essen, Städtische Bühne: *The Brig* (1)

22, Bonn, Universität Hörsaal: *Maids* (1); *Mysteries* (1)

23, Heidelberg, Schloss, Königsaal: *Maids* (1); *Mysteries* (1)

29, Vienna, Theater an der Wien: *Mysteries* (1)

30-December 2, *The Brig* (3)

December 2, Vienna, Haus der Jugend: *Mysteries* (1) Followed by discussion.

5, Malmö, Stadsteater, Intiman: *Maids* (2)

6, *Mysteries* (1)

7, Lund, Stora Salen, Akademiska Føreningen, Universitat: *Mysteries* (1)

9, Göteborg, Stadsteater: *Mysteries* (1); Intiman: *Maids* (1)

12-13, Stockholm, Marionetteatern: *Maids* (2)

14-15, *Mysteries* (2)

16, Uppsala, Stadsteater: *Mysteries* (1)

18, Helsinki, Stadsteater: *Maids* (1)

19, Helsinki, Soumen Kansallisteatteri: *Mysteries* (1)

21, Stockholm, Marionnetteatern: *Maids* (1); *Mysteries* (1)

25, Copenhagen, Det Kongelige Teater: *Mysteries* (1)

28-29, Copenhagen, Fiol Teater: *Maids* (2)

30, Copenhagen, Det ny Scala: *Mysteries* (1)

1966

January 1, Aarhuis (Denmark), Aarhuis Theater: *Maids* (1)

2, *Mysteries* (1)

21-30, Bologna, Teatro Stabile al Teatro Apollo: *The Brig* (10)

February 2-6, Milan, Palazzo Durini: *Mysteries* (7)

17, Milan, Università Politecnica: *Mysteries* (1)

21, Genoa, Auditorium della Fiera della Mare: *Mysteries* (1)

23, Lecco, Salone Don Rodrigo: *Mysteries* (1)

24-March 7, Venice, Teatro del Ridotto: *Mysteries* (5)

March 3-6, Catania, Palazzo Biscari-Moncada: *Mysteries* (4)

11, Catania, Istituto del Magistero della Università: *Mysteries* (1)

19-20, Bari, Teatro Piccinni: *Mysteries* (2)

29, Sarajevo, Narodno Pozoriste: *The Brig* (1)

30, Sarajevo, Festival Malih i Scena experimentalnih: *Mysteries* (2)

April 1, Sarajevo, Workers Theatre: *The Brig* (1)

    2, Mostar (Yugoslavia), Narodno Pozoriste: *Mysteries* (1)

    3, Zenica (Yugoslavia), Narodno Pozoriste: *Mysteries* (1)

    4, Banja Luca (Yugoslavia), Dom Kulture: *Mysteries* (1)

    15-17, Modena, Teatro Comunale: *The Brig* (3)

    21, Reggio-Emilia, Teatro Municipale: *The Brig* (1)

    22-27, Bologna, Teatro Stabile al Teatro Apollo: *Mysteries* (6)

    30, Ferrara, Teatro Comunale: *The Brig* (1)

May 4, Parma, Teatro Comunale-Regio: *The Brig* (1)

    5-8, Turin, Unione Culturale, Palazzo Carignano: *Mysteries* (4)

    21, Trente, Teatro Sociale: *Mysteries* (1)

    22, Rimini, Teatro Novelli: *Mysteries* (1)

    30. Milan, Palazzo Durini: *Free Theatre* (1)

June 10, Reggio-Emilia, Circolo Gramsci: *Mysteries* (1)

    27-28, Paris, Odéon Théâtre de France: *The Brig* (2)

    29-30 *Mysteries* (2)

July 29, Cassis, Festival de Cassis, Grand Théâtre: *Frankenstein* (1)

August 2 and 5, *Frankenstein* (2)

August 4, *Mysteries* (1)

September 1-10, Berlin, Akademie der Künste: *The Brig* (10)

    28-*October* 2, *Frankenstein* (5)

October 7-11, *Maids* (3); *Mysteries* (3)

    12-13, *Frankenstein* (2)

    14-15, *Maids* (2)

    23-25, Venice, Teatro del Ridotto: *Maids* (3)

    26-31, *Mysteries* (6)

November 1, Trente, Università Sociologica: *Mysteries* (1)

3-5, Turin, Unione Culturale, Palazzo Carignano: *Maids* (4)
9-12, Brussels, Théâtre 140: *Frankenstein* (4)
15-17, Amsterdam, Sigma Centrum, Voormalige
Doelenzaal: *Maids* (3)
19, Enschede, De Twentse Schouwburg: *Frankenstein* (1)
21-22, Amsterdam, Sigma Centrum, Voormalige
Doelenzaal: *Maids* (2)
23, Rotterdam, De Rotterdamse Stadsschouwburg: *Mysteries* (1)
24-25, Amsterdam, Sigma Centrum, Voormalige
Doelenzaal: *Maids* (2)
26-29, *Mysteries* (4)
December 1-4, Brussels, Théâtre 140: *Frankenstein*
(2)
7-8, Amsterdam, Théâtre Carré: *Frankenstein*
(2)
10, Nijmegen, Stadsschouwburg: *Frankenstein*
(1)
11, Esslingen, Stadttheater Württ, Landesbühne:
Mysteries (1)
12, Laren, Singer Memorial Concertzaal: *Mysteries* (1)
14, Utrecht, Stadsschouwburg: *Mysteries* (1)
16-17, Haarlem, Stadsschouwburg: *The Brig* (2)
19, Tilburg, Stadsschouwburg: *The Brig* (1)
20, Eindhoven, Stadsschouwburg: *Mysteries* (1)
22, Maastricht, Stadsschouwburg: *Frankenstein*
(1)
24-29, Amsterdam, Sigma Centrum, Voormalige
Doelenzaal: *Mysteries* (5)

1967

January 1-2, Braunschweig, Staatstheater, Kleines
Haus: *Mysteries* (2)
2-3, Hannover, Humboldtschule-Landestheater:
Mysteries (2)

5, Wesel, Städtliche Bühne: *Mysteries* (1)

7-8, Munich, Theater in der Brienner Strasse: *Frankenstein* (2)

9-13, *Mysteries* (5)

15, Heidelberg, Städtische Bühne: *Frankenstein* (1)

18, Frankfort, Cantatesaal Theater: *Mysteries* (1)

20, Mannheim, Nationaltheater, Kleines Haus: *Mysteries* (1)

21, Frankfort, Cantatesaal: *Maids* (1); *Mysteries* (1)

22, *Mysteries* (1)

23, Bern, Alhambra-Saal (Hôtel National): *Mysteries* (1)

30-February 3, Frankfort, Theater am Turm: *Frankenstein* (2)

February 6, Hamburg, Auditorium Maximum: *Frankenstein* (1)

7, *Maids* (1); *Mysteries* (1)

8, *The Brig* (1)

18-19, Krefeld, Stadttheater: *Antigone* (2) Opening.

21, Mönchen-Gladbach, Stadttheater: *Mysteries* (1)

23, Oberhausen, Städtische Bühne: *Frankenstein* (1)

24, Dinslaken, Festhalle des Gymnasium in der Hagenstrasse: *Antigone* (1)

25, Krefeld, Stadttheater: *Frankenstein* (1)

26, Bad Godesberg, Stadthalle: *Antigone* (1)

March 1, Cologne-Mühlheim, Stadthalle: *Antigone* (1)

3-4, Hamburg, Theater am Besenbindorf: *The Brig* (2)

5, Kiel, Stadttheater: *Antigone* (1)

7-9, Geneva, Théâtre de Carouge: *Mysteries* (2)

8-10, *Antigone* (2)

11, Geneva, Théâtre de la Comédie: *Mysteries* (1)

13-16, Turin, Unione Culturale: *Antigone* (3);
  Piper Club: *Mysteries* (1)
19, Parma, Teatro Regio: *Antigone* (1)
27, Perugia, Teatro Morlacchi: *World Action*
  (1)
28, *Mysteries* (1)
29, *Antigone* (1)
April 3, L'Aquila, Teatro Comunale: *Antigone* (1)
  5-9, Rome, Teatro Delle Arti: *Antigone* (3);
    Maids (2)
  11-12, Genoa, Teatro Stabile, Sala Politeama
    genovese: *Antigone* (2)
  13-14, *Frankenstein* (2)
  15, *Maids* (1)
  17-*May* 1, Milan, Palazzo Durini: *Antigone*
    (9); *Maids* (8)
May 2, Modena, Teatro Comunale: *Frankenstein* (1)
  4, Carpi, Teatro Comunale: *Frankenstein* (1)
  5-7, Turin, Teatro Alfieri: *Frankenstein* (3)
  9, Prato, Teatro Metastasio: *Antigone* (1)
  10-13, Rome, Teatro Parioli: *Mysteries* (3);
    Antigone (3)
  14, *Antigone* (1); *Maids* (1)
  16, Reggio-Emilia, Teatro Municipale: *Antig-
    one* (1)
  17, Ferrara, Teatro Comunale: *Antigone* (1)
  20, Bari, Teatro Piccinni: *Antigone* (1)
  21, *Frankenstein* (1)
  23, Naples, Teatro Politeama: *Frankenstein* (1)
  24, *Antigone* (1)
  27, Salerno, Teatro Augusteo: *Mysteries* (1)
  29, Leghorn, Casa della Cultura: *Antigone* (1)
  30, Florence, Teatro Andrea del Sarto: *Antig-
    one* (1)
  31, Sienna, Teatro Rinovata: *Mysteries* (1)
June 6, Caen, Maison de la Culture: *The Brig* (1)
  7, *Mysteries* (1)
  8-9, *Frankenstein* (2)
  10, *Maids* (1)
August 3-5, Paris, Studio 102, ORTF: *Mysteries* (3)

September 6-22, Paris, Théâtre Alpha 347: *Mysteries* (18)

24-25, Belgrade, Atelier 212: *Antigone* (3)

October 3-5, Dublin, Olympia Theatre: *Frankenstein* (3)

6-8, *Antigone* (3)

13-22, Brussels, Théâtre 140: *Antigone* (9)

23-24, Liège, Palais des Congrès: *Antigone* (2)

26, Seraing, Centre Cultural Communal: *Antigone* (2)

November 3-5, Barcelona, Teatre Romea: *Antigone* (4)

7, Valladolid, Teatro Carrion: *Antigone* (1)

8, Bilbao, Teatre Campos Eliseos: *Antigone* (1)

9, San Sebastian, Teatro Victoria Eugenia: *Antigone* (1)

13, Bordeaux, Théâtre Français: *Antigone* (1)

17, *All'Italia* (1)

18, *Mysteries* (1)

20, Bordeaux, Théâtre Alhambra: *Frankenstein* (1)

23-26, Paris, Theatre Alpha 347: *Antigone* (4)

27, Nanterre, Faculté des Lettres, Grand Amphithéâtre: *Mysteries* (1)

28-*December* 3, Paris, Théâtre Alpha 347: *Antigone* (6)

December 4, Paris, Faculté de Droit: *Antigone* (1)

5-31, Paris, Théâtre Alpha 347; *Antigone* (24)

1968

January 6, Geneva, Grand Théâtre: *Frankenstein* (1)

9, Lausanne, Théâtre Municipal: *Frankenstein* (1)

10, *Antigone* (1)

11, Bern, Stadttheater: *Antigone* (1)

15, Lucerne, Stadttheater: *Mysteries* (1)

16, Zürich, Theater im Volkshaus: *Antigone* (1)

17, *Frankenstein* (1)

18, *Mysteries* (1)

19, *Antigone* (1)

20, Geneva, Théâtre de la Comédie: *Mysteries* (1)

21-22, *Antigone* (2)

25, Zürich, Theater im Volkshaus: *Antigone* (1)

26, *Mysteries* (1)

May 2-3, Palermo, Teatro Mobile Popolare—Zappalà nei Giardini Inglesi: *Mysteries* (2)

10, Bourges, Maison de la Culture: *Antigone* (1)

11, Tours, Palais des Sports: *Antigone* (1)

July 20, Avignon, Cloître des Carmes (Festival d'Avignon): *Antigone* (1)

22, *Mysteries* (1)

24-26, *Paradise Now* (3) Opening.

August 1, Ollioules (Festival de Chateauvallon, near Toulon): *Paradise Now* (1) Free performance.

20-24, Geneva, Pavillon des Sports: *Paradise Now* (5)

September 3, on board the *S.S. Aurelia,* crossing the Atlantic (lat. 49º 01′ N, long. 25º 21′ W), the Riviera Lounge: *Mysteries* (1)

B. AMERICAN TOUR, *1968-1969*

September 16-18, 21, New Haven, Yale University Theatre: *Mysteries* (4) (21: free performance)

19-21, *Antigone* (3)

23-25, *Frankenstein* (3)

26-28, *Paradise Now* (3)

October 2-7, New York City, Brooklyn Academy of Music, Music Hall: *Frankenstein* (6)

9-20, *Mysteries* (5)

10-19, *Antigone* (5)

14-21, *Paradise Now* (6)

22, New York City, Fillmore East: first rung of *Paradise Now* (1)

28, Stony Brook, New York University, gymnasium: *Mysteries* (1)

29, *Paradise Now* (1)

31-November 1, Cambridge, Mass., Kresge Auditorium: *Frankenstein* (2)

November 2, *Antigone* (1)

3, *Mysteries* (2)

5, *Paradise Now* (1)

12, Plainfield, Vt., Goddard College, Haybarn Theatre: *Mysteries* (1)

14, Pittsburgh, Pa., Carnegie-Mellon University, Skibo Hall: *Mysteries* (1)

15, *Paradise Now* (1)

18, New Brunswick, N.J., Rutgers University, Hickman Hall: *The Rite of Guerilla Theatre* (1) First lecture-demonstration.

20, Castleton, Vt., Castleton College, gymnasium: *Paradise Now* (1)

21, Bennington, Vt., Bennington College, gymnasium: *Paradise Now* (1)

22, Northampton, Mass., Smith College, John M. Greene Hall: *Guerilla Theatre* (1) Lecture-demonstration.

24-26, Philadelphia, YMHA, Fleischer Auditorium: *Antigone* (1); *Frankenstein* (1); *Paradise Now* (1)

27, Philadelphia, Temple University, Tomlinson Theater: *The Rite of Guerilla Theatre* (1) Lecture-demonstration.

30, Princeton, N.J., Princeton University, McCarter Theater: *Mysteries* (1)

December 1, Great Neck, N.Y., Beth-El Auditorium: *Antigone* (1)

2, Scranton, Pa., University of Scranton, Long Center Gymnasium: *Mysteries* (1)

4, Granville, Ohio, Denison University, gymnasium: *Mysteries* (1)

6-7, Cincinnati, Ohio, Playhouse in the Park:

Frankenstein (1); *Mysteries* (1);   *Antigone* (1)

10-11, Ann Arbor, Mich., Michigan Union Ballroom: *Mysteries* (1); *Paradise Now* (1)

12-14, Detroit, Mich., Detroit Art Institute, Auditorium: *Mysteries* (1); *Antigone* (1); *Frankenstein* (1)

16-18, Ithaca, N.Y., Cornell University, Bailey Hall: *Mysteries* (1); *Paradise Now* (1)

17, Rochester, N.Y., University of Rochester, Strong Auditorium; *Paradise Now* (1)

21-22, Boston, Mass. (Roxbury), Crown Manor: *Antigone* (1); *Paradise Now* (1)

24-*January* 1, New York City (Bronx), Poe Forum: *Frankenstein* (3); *Mysteries* (2); *Antigone* (1); *Paradise Now* (2)

January 2-4, New York City, Hunter College, Concert Hall: *Antigone* (1); *Mysteries* (1); *Paradise Now* (1)

7-12, Chicago, University of Chicago, Mandel Hall: *Mysteries* (2); *Antigone* (1); *Frankenstein* (2); *Paradise Now* (1)

15-16, Madison, Wis., First Unitarian Church, Meeting House: *Antigone* (1); *Paradise Now* (1)

17-18, Appleton, Wis., Lawrence Memorial Chapel: *Mysteries* (1); *Frankenstein* (1)

22, Iowa City, Iowa, Iowa Memorial Union, Grand Ballroom: *Mysteries* (1); *Antigone* (1)

24, Chicago, The Auditorium Theatre: *Paradise Now* (1)

28-31, Kansas City, Kansas, Soldiers and Sailors Memorial: *Mysteries* (1); *Antigone* (1); *Paradise Now* (1)

February 2, Hays, Kansas, Sheridan Coliseum: *Mysteries* (1)

4, Fort Collins, Colo., Center Theatre: *Antigone* (1)

5-6, Boulder, Colo., University of Colorado,
Macky Auditorium: *Frankenstein* (1)
UMC Ballroom: *Paradise Now* (1)
11-15, Portland, Ore., Reed College, Sports
Center: *Mysteries* (2); *Paradise Now* (1);
The Commons: *Antigone* (1)
16, Ashland, Ore., Southern Oregon College,
Churchill Hall: *Antigone* (1)
18-20, Berkeley, Calif., Berkeley Community
Theatre: *Mysteries* (1); *Frankenstein* (1);
Paradise Now (1)
24-28, Los Angeles, Calif., University of Southern California: *The Rite of Guerilla Theatre* (1) Lecture-demonstration; Bovard
Auditorium: *Mysteries* (1); *Frankenstein*
(2); *Antigone* (1); *Paradise Now* (1)
March 4-10, San Francisco, Calif., Straight Theatre:
The Rite of Opposite Forces (1) free performance; *The Brig Dollar* (1) free performance; Nourse Auditorium: *Antigone*
(1); *Frankenstein* (1); *Paradise Now* (1)
8, Oakland, Calif., Mills College, Concert Hall:
The Rite of Guerilla Theatre (1) Lecture-
demonstration.
19-20, Boston, Mass., The Ark: *Mysteries* (1);
Antigone (1)
21, New York City, Theatre of Ideas, *Guerilla Theatre* (1)
28-29, New York City, Brooklyn Academy of
Music, Music Hall: *Paradise Now* (4);
Antigone (1); Opera House: *Frankenstein* (3); Brooklyn College, Walt Whitman Hall: *Mysteries* (1)

C. European Tours, *1969-1970*

April 16, Chambéry, Théâtre Charles Dullin: *Mysteries* (1)
18, Dijon, Grand Théâtre: *Mysteries* (1)

25-27, Lille, Théâtre Municipal (Opéra de Lille): *Mysteries* (3)

29-*May* 1, Mulhouse, Salle du Rallye Drouot (Théâtre du Mercredi): *Mysteries* (1); *Antigone* (1); *Paradise Now* (1) Free performance.

May 6, Saint-Hilaire du Touvet, Théâtre du Sanatorium des Étudiants: *Paradise Now* (1)

7-10, Grenoble, Maison de la Culture: *Mysteries* (2); *Antigone* (2)

10, Saint Martin d'Hères, Terrasse de la Bibliothèque des Faculté de Droit et Lettres, Université de Grenoble. *Paradise Now* (1) Free performance

12, Albi, Théâtre Municipal: *Antigone* (1)

13-25, Toulouse, Théâtre Daniel Sorano: *Mysteries* (6); *Antigone* (6): Cité Universitaire garden: For Toulouse (1) free performance.

27-28, Lyon, Théâtre du VIIIème: *Mysteries* (1); *Antigone* (1)

29-31, Saint Étienne, Comédie de Saint-Étienne, Salle des Mutilés: *Mysteries* (1); *Antigone* (1); *Paradise Now* (1)

June 4-28, London, The Roundhouse: *Frankenstein* (8); *Mysteries* (4); *Paradise Now* (6); *Antigone* (3)

August 31, Essaouira, Morocco: Excerpts from *Paradise Now: The Rite of Opposite Forces, Mysteries: The Chord,* (1) free performance.

27-*September* 30, Taormina, Teatro Greco-romano: *Antigone* (3); *Mysteries* (1)

October 2, Caltanisetta, Supercinema: *Antigone* (1)

10-16, Venice, Teatro del Ridotto: *Antigone* (5); *Mysteries* (2)

18, Brescia, Teatro Comunale Santa Chiara: *Antigone* (1)

20-21, Turin, Teatro Alfieri: *Paradise Now*

(1); Unione Culturale, Palazzo Carignano:
Paradise Now (1)

23-24, Brescia, Teatro Communale Santa
Chiara: *Mysteries* (2)

25-*November* 2, Milan, Circo Medini: *Mysteries* (3); *Antigone* (2); *Paradise Now* (1);
Università Politecnica: *Paradise Now* (1)

November 6, Ferrara, Teatro Comunale: *Mysteries*
(1)

7-9, Bologna, Teatro La Ribalta: *Antigone* (3)

10, Capri, Teatro Comunale: *Antigone* (1)

11, Bologna, Aula Magna dell' Università: *The
Rite of Guerilla Theatre* (1), free performance.

11, Modena, Teatro Communale: *Antigone* (1)

12, Reggio Emilia, Teatro Communale: *Antigone* (1)

14-16, Prato, Teatro Metastasio: *Paradise Now*
(3)

17-18, Florence, Space Electronic: *Mysteries*
(1); *Paradise Now* (1)

20-21, Urbino, Supercinema Ducale: *Antigone*
(1); Cellar of the Teatro Sanzio: *Paradise
Now* (1)

23, Pesaro, Teatro Sperimentale: *Mysteries* (1)

29-30, Naples, Teatro Mediterraneo: *Paradise
Now* (2)

December 1, Rome, Università di Roma, Facoltà
di Legge: *Paradise Now* (1)

8-9, Louvain, Stadsschouwburg Leuven: *Mysteries* (1): Centre Culturel: *Mysteries* (1)

10-13, Bruxelles, Théâtre 140: *Paradise Now*
(4)

15-16, Seraing, Centre Culturel: *Mysteries* (1);
Paradise Now (1)

18-23, Bruxelles, Théâtre 140: *Mysteries* (3);
Paradise Now (3)

31-*Jan.* 11, *1970*, Berlin, Akademie der Künste:
Paradise Now (2); *Mysteries* (2); *Antigone*
(3); Sportpalast: *Paradise Now* (1).

THE COMPANY
(Spring, 1969)

United States: Julian Beck, Judith Malina, James Anderson, Cal Barber, Carol Berger, Melvin Clay, Rufus Collins, Carl Einhorn, Gene Gordon, Roy Harris, Jenny Hecht, Henry Howard, Nona Howard, Steven Ben Israel, Mary Mary, William Shari, Dorothy Shari, Steve Thompson, Jim Tiroff, Luke Theodore, Diana Van Tosh, Peter Weiss, Karen Weiss. *West Germany:* Birgit Knabe, Gunter Pannewitz, Petra Vogt. *Holland:* Frank Hoogeboom, Sandy Linden, Margery Barber. *Italy:* Gianfranco Mantegna, Leo Treviglio. *France:* Odile Bingisser. *Great Britain:* Rodney Beere. *Australia:* Pamela Badyk. *Austria:* Echnaton.

INDEX